I0759411

There Is No Other

Also by Ram Dass

Identification and Child Rearing
The Psychedelic Experience
LSD
Be Here Now
Doing Your Own Being
The Only Dance There Is
Grist for the Mill
Journey of Awakening
Miracle of Love
How Can I Help?
Compassion in Action
Still Here
Paths to God
Be Love Now
Polishing the Mirror
Walking Each Other Home
Being Ram Dass

THERE IS NO OTHER

The Way to Harmony and Wholeness

RAM DASS

Edited by PARVATI MARKUS

REFLECTIONS AND PRACTICES from
SHARON SALZBERG, JOSEPH GOLDSTEIN,
JACK KORNFIELD, and MIRABAI BUSH

HARPERONE
An Imprint of HarperCollins*Publishers*

HarperCollins books may be purchased for educational, business, or sales promotional use. For information, please email the Special Markets Department at SPsales@harpercollins.com.

harpercollins.com

FIRST EDITION

Designed by Nancy Singer

Library of Congress Cataloging-in-Publication Data has been applied for.

ISBN 978-0-06-344302-0

25 26 27 28 29 LBC 5 4 3 2 1

To Neem Karoli Baba, who shows us the reality of

sub ek, all one.

And to Ram Dass for leading us on the journey to get there.

Contents

Part II
SELF-AWARENESS

Part III
COMING INTO WHOLENESS

Foreword

by Anne Lamott

It's human nature to take sides and to think that you're right and that you speak for God. My great Jesuit friend, Tom Weston, said you can tell you've created God in your own image when he or she hates all the same people you do. So that's always a very good hint that you're a little off track. We're taught black and white, and what has gotten a lot of us into trouble is this black-and-white thinking, this win-and-lose consciousness. Much of social life isn't split into black and white. Real life has got subtleties and layers and complexities and nuance.

There are two ways nowadays of looking at a stranger. When you're distrustful of somebody, you think they're going to take your food or your car or your right to vote or whatever, so you have the right to punish them and exclude them. Your instinct tells you that you have to for your own survival. Or they've come here to trade with you, and you have the right to be involved.

It's a transaction, so you have to make sure they don't cheat you and that they accept returns. We don't entirely trust anyone outside of our households and our sacred communities.

We have fences and private properties and envy and a general sense that the people who live next door and definitely the people who vote differently than we do are not our tribe. So we're still worried they're going to steal from us, they're going to bargain unfairly with us, and we're going to come out on the losing end.

We develop these beliefs about danger and we end up growing into these political, religious, and other social polarizations. It's very deep in us. On top of that fear is the shame of discovering you secretly have a lot of beliefs that are polarized and prejudiced. There should be no shame in this—our culture and families bred it into us. An acronym for shame is Should Have Already Mastered Everything. Good luck with that! The opposite of shame is to understand that we are works in progress (please be patient) and that in everything there is subtlety, there is compromise, and there is nuance. It's complicated here.

It really helps to take our belief systems a little more lightly. I can't possibly be right because I can't see the future. I have no idea what the overall picture is from the species point of view. I only think I do. In fact, I'm positive I do. I'm just positive, positive, positive that my beliefs and opinions are right. So I close my eyes and pray to God: "I am in too deep a hole. I could use your help getting out of this stuck-ness and this prejudice and this shutdown-ness and moving into grace and gentleness and open-mindedness. Thank you in advance for your healing and tender mercies. Amen."

I also read beautiful works on truth and reconciliation and compassion, everything by Ram Dass and Jack Kornfield and Sharon Salzberg about pure and radical coming together in total love with people who are so different from us.

Another thing I do is recognize that this indignation and contempt are of no use to me. In fact, they're toxic. They are guaranteed to make me mentally sick and spiritually off, rashy on the inside. If I fall into them, I'm going to want to catch myself. I'm going to pray for God to help me. I'm going to read really deep spiritual stuff and I'm going to try and take my beliefs lightly. There's a great line in the AA Big Book where Bill Wilson urges sober alcoholics to avoid the "deliberate manufacture of misery." This means no doomscrolling, no reading things where people brilliantly articulate my bad, contemptuous, shut-down-heart views on what's going on politically and socially.

Instead, I read C. S. Lewis. I read the poets Mary Oliver and W. S. Merwin. I read Robert Thurman. I immerse myself in truth and beauty and goodness, "goodness" being a synonym for God. I turn away from this dark thought process. I choose grace. Grace is spiritual WD-40. I use it to unclench. What happens then is I breathe in, I breathe out. I go left foot, right foot, left foot, breathe.

Martin Luther King Jr. said something that has helped me almost more than anything. He said, "Let no man pull you so low as to hate him." Hate steals away the power of your love and the truth of your spiritual identity, which is that you are love, you are goodness, you're a sweet, curious child filled with wonder and curiosity. These darker personas and positions were all added to us by our parents and our teachers who were afraid, who wanted us to stay alive and to believe what they believed so that it would prove that they were right. Well, as the Buddhists say, do you want to be happy or do you want to be right? I kind of want to be right, but more than anything, I want to *be*.

I think about how the benefits of doing this work on your own divisive thoughts, your own polarized feelings shared by half the nation, maybe people in your own family, are enormous. I want to be free. I want to be God's love in expression. That is why I've been reading Ram Dass since I was twenty. I always keep a copy of *Be Here Now* around. I pray and I meditate and I teach and I listen. I want to be free. I want to be here now. I want to be me. I want to be the me I was born to be, free and curious and full of wonder and kind of goofy. I want to be walking in the woods instead of strategizing about winning or needing to correct people and needing to be right. I don't want to be divided anymore.

My understanding of grace in the Christian tradition is that God loves my worst political opponent exactly the same as he or she loves the newest baby at church. That's the mystery of grace.

It's really hard here on this side of eternity, on the incarnation side of things. Meister Eckhart said that if the soul could have known God without the world, God would never have created the world. We have the opportunity to get closer to God by doing that radical work that brings us into union both with ourselves and with God and the world.

When it comes to polarization and divisiveness, the thing to remember is that our greatest strength is our vulnerability. And what that looks like is being willing to surrender to a power greater than ourselves. A great acronym for God, besides Good Orderly Direction and Grace Over Drama, is GUS, Great Universal Spirit. We practice surrendering to GUS and putting down our weapons. Our weapons have to do with the illusions of being right and believing that certain behaviors make us safe. We're obviously not right all the time, and we're as vulnerable as kittens on this side of eternity. So you put down your weapons and come over to the winning side, which is peace and love. That means that you trust people's innate goodness and develop a willingness to get to know them and listen. Maybe the hardness is going to melt in their hearts, and they're going to be able to sit down with you and see that you're not a communist baby killer but a mom, or a sister or brother, or a grandpa or auntie.

I keep bringing my mind back to "trust and surrender." Trust and surrender. I'm in charge of almost nothing but helping the animals get fed because they don't have opposable thumbs and can't work the can opener. The rest I try to leave in God's good hands, and live—or try to live—by our sister Valarie Kaur's words: *See No Stranger*, as well as we can, one day at a time.

Introduction

by Parvati Markus

I was at the winter 2019 Open Your Heart in Paradise retreat in Maui, the last one Ram Dass attended in person; he left his body only weeks after it ended. We'd come a long way since the first time I met him at his father's home in New Hampshire in the summer of 1969, a year after he had met Maharajji, Neem Karoli Baba, in India. I was blown away by the light that emanated from him. I was speechless. How could someone radiate that much light? What did he know, what did he have, what did he have access to that was so different from what I had available to me? The light that was coming from this other being was filled with excitement, with anticipation, with the demand that I seek its source.

Two years later, in September 1971, I was riding in Ram Dass's VW bus from the Hotel Evelyn in Nainital, in the foothills of the Himalayas, to Neem Karoli Baba's ashram at Kainchi to meet his (and my) guru. It was an extraordinary time—basking in the presence of Maharajji and experiencing the grace of unconditional love. In March 1972, we left India on the same plane (with a stop in Italy that gave us the chance to grab a bowl of pasta). Those of us who were part of that wave of Westerners with Maharajji have a deep sense of connection with one another and with Ram Dass. We are satsang, as the community of spiritual seekers is called in Hinduism ("sangha" in Buddhism).

Fifty years after our first meeting, as the retreat in Maui was drawing to a close, Ram Dass and I connected across a room. The powerful light that came from those magnetic blue eyes was the same light I had seen in 1969, and my goodbye was as speechless as my first encounter with him had been. No words were necessary. He was not "other" than me; there was nothing but the wholeness of love.

And then he was gone.

The good news is that Ram Dass left us with an overflowing archive of talks and lectures, books and courses, interviews and collaborations. His wisdom is still available to us. We can hang out with him, enjoying his sense of humor as well as benefiting from his profound insights into human nature and our spiritual aspirations. We can dig into his words when we have a problem we're wrestling with or a heart that needs to open or if we just want his hand to hold as we stumble along on our individual paths.

These days we are collectively in need of healing the terrible divide within our society. What can we do to relieve the pain of living with hatred or fear or dissatisfaction with the "other," either the others we see as destroying the world or the other parts of ourselves that are destroying our inner peace and harmony? Maybe you are in unrelenting pain and the only way out is to have your consciousness immersed in an addiction—drugs or alcohol (or both), food, pornography, gambling, gaming, social media, TV bingeing, or anything that has the power to distract you from the divisions within yourself and in the world around you. Maybe you feel your heart closing down. Maybe you're living in fear. Maybe you're wondering how you can live in peace with those whose beliefs are so very different from yours.

Ram Dass was no stranger to "us" versus "them." In *Be Here Now*, he defined that polarization as "Hippies create police; police create hippies. If you're in polarity, you're creating polar opposites." Ram Dass didn't run from the contrasting forces of good and evil, yes and no, pleasure and pain, loss and gain. He didn't complain on social media. He didn't lecture against anything or anyone. He didn't ask his followers to vote for a certain party or stick to a particular spiritual path. Instead, he dove into his guru's instructions to *love everyone*. He put a framed picture of the person who most represented the polar opposite of his personal beliefs on his altar, right next to the images of his guru and other beings who point the way to oneness. And he would try to open his heart to love the "other" as a soul, not as the role they played in society.

In his early life as Richard Alpert, as a Harvard professor of psychology, Ram Dass was fascinated with the mind. His academic career came to a close when he and his colleague Timothy Leary were fired from Harvard for their explorations into the outer reaches of the mind through psilocybin and LSD, and he wound up in India where he met his guru, Neem Karoli Baba. There he absorbed Maharajji's oft-repeated teaching: *sub ek*, all one. "Many names, many forms . . . sub ek, all one."

There is no higher or lower, no earthly versus spiritual planes, no "us" versus "them." It's all one whole.

Wholeness

What does it mean to be whole? We live our lives as if we were distinct parts, separate from one another no matter how much like family we may feel. Our separateness is an illusion, but it's a powerful one. Your body is separate from mine, your religion is different, your politics are different, your heritage is different. How can we be one whole?

We're separate not only from one another but also from ourselves. We think of ourselves as separate from our own divinity—the place where, as the Indian saint Ramana Maharshi put it, God, guru, and self are one. And because we think we are separate and feel alone in our separateness, we suffer.

What does "wholeness" mean? It can be defined as the quality of being or feeling complete, not divided or damaged in any way. A *whole*-body approach to health includes the body, mind, emotions, and spirit. A *wholeness* center is a place that integrates traditional health care with more nonconventional methods, like nutritional therapy, psychedelic-assisted therapy, brain mapping, neurofeedback, and other modalities for a holistic body-mind approach to healing. After having a severe stroke, Ram Dass spent the last twenty-two years of his life bringing his constant physical pain into harmony with spirit, into the loving awareness he cultivated deep within his being.

But how do we come to know everything as a whole? How do we embody unity within ourselves? How do we get to the place where our self-hatred and our self-love come into union?

How can we recognize the oppositions we live with inside and outside ourselves and learn to see all sides as one? This is the work of becoming whole as an individual and as a society.

"Wholeness" doesn't mean adhering to any one set of similarities. In the US, we are far from being all white, male, heterosexual, and Christian. It is projected that the US population will be less than half white by 2045. Is there a way to view us as we are—composed of all races, all gender permutations, all sexual possibilities, all religious and cultural values and expressions? Can we learn to see into the complex divisions we have set up in our minds and hearts?

In his inimitable style, Ram Dass takes us through the divisions and separations we harbor and brings us into a reconciliation of opposing forces, the differences that separate us from others and from our true nature. Hopefully one day we will be able to hold within ourselves the full spectrum of humanity and our own beliefs and behaviors. Certainly life as an individual would benefit greatly. Indeed, life on earth may depend on it.

In This Book

Maybe you have become mindful of your conflicting thoughts and emotions and want to know how to get past them into a place of higher consciousness, into unity consciousness. That's what we're doing here. We look to Ram Dass's teachings to help us mend the torn fabric of our lives and times.

Here, Ram Dass encourages us to move from role to soul and find our identity in a polarized world. We learn to go beyond judgment and cultivate compassion for those who hold beliefs and perspectives that differ from our own. We listen to stories, told by the master storyteller himself, that lift us from our daily concerns about ourselves into the realm of community/satsang/sangha and pull us toward unity. We see how the illusion of the separate self evaporates in the truth of our interconnection. We see Maharajji pointing upward with one finger and understand that sub ek, all one, is where we're headed.

Ram Dass's exploration and teachings on polarity are much needed these days, when the whole world seems to teeter between one pole and the other. In this book, Ram Dass shows us how a house divided against itself—whether that "house" is our individual selves or the society in which we live—can come together in wholeness.

I will be your guide, introducing each chapter to provide context for the material. The teachings I included in this book were culled and consolidated from more than fifty different lectures Ram Dass gave across the country. There were times when he would speak at sixty different cities on a single tour! They range from his classic talks at Yale University and the New York Sculpture Studio in the sixties to talks he gave at retreats in Maui in the 2000s. For a complete list of these resources, see page 259. I also took some material from an unpublished interview Raghu Markus and David Silver did with Ram Dass in 2018, called "The Habit of Honesty," and used some of Ram Dass's comments from interviews I did with him for my book *Love Everyone.*

In part 1, we look through Ram Dass's eyes at the ways in which we view others as "them" and the reasons behind that type of thinking, like how we cling to our thoughts and beliefs and how we judge others and ourselves. He offers us ways to get beyond judgment and attachment and leads us to the path of mindful service.

In part 2, we travel from head to heart, from role to soul, from there to here and then to now. But first we have to understand what the journey is that will take us beyond our separate identities and our suffering and allow us to feel whole, and so Ram Dass offers an overview of the spiritual journey.

In part 3, Ram Dass helps us navigate the ocean of wholeness and shows us the support we have in this pursuit, from our gurus and teachers to our spiritual community.

Through excerpts from his countless lectures, many of which have never been published before, through quotes from a few of his books, such as *Polishing the Mirror* and *Being Ram Dass*, and with a little help from his friends—our "cousins" Sharon Salzberg, Jack Kornfield, and Joseph Goldstein from the Buddhist community, who often taught with Ram Dass, and one of Ram Dass's frequent collaborators and friend, Mirabai Bush—Ram Dass shows us how we can come to know that there is no "other."

It's just us.

Sub Ek

Maharajji often pointed the way for us to go beyond the duality of the world, beyond our inner heart-mind duality, by raising one finger. Depending on your state of mind at the moment, you might take the gesture as a warning sign, like "Watch out!" Be that as it may, it was also a clear gesture indicating sub ek, all one.

He'd ask us Westerners, "What's the difference between Ram and Christ?"

We'd respond, "They're one."

He'd point upward. "Do you understand?"

He'd ask, "What's the difference between God and guru?"

"They're one."

"Sub ek. All are one. Love everyone. See all as the same."

Ram Dass saw it this way. . . .

Maharajji's statement, sub ek, has been my saving grace. Sub ek—there's only one. It's all one. All one.

Now, you and I can sit around and discuss whether the One and the zero are the same thing, or whether the One is an illusion. But from my point of view, from where my work is, I am reassuringly helped a lot by remembering the reality of the One.

I had a dialogue once with Chögyam Trungpa Rinpoche in front of some television cameras when Trungpa was teaching a seminar on Don Juan in Vermont. He said to me, "Ram Dass, what do you do about sorcerers?"

I said, "What sorcerers? I don't see any sorcerers."

"Don't cop out. What do you do about sorcerers?"

I said, "I don't notice all that stuff. It's none of my business. I'm just aiming for the One."

PART I

There Is No "Other"

Disregarding our tendency to see people in terms of "us" and "them," we should recognize that actually they are just like us. All eight billion of us have to live together helping each other as best we can.

—*His Holiness the 14th Dalai Lama*

Chapter 1

"Us" Versus "Them"

If we are not yet enlightened (and, really, who among us is living in the wholeness of who we are?), then we are living in separation and polarity. There's me and there's you, my karma versus your karma, my desires versus your desires. I'm right; you're wrong. Collectively, there's us *and there's* them, *our people versus your people, our team against your team.*

But Maharajji held one finger in the air and said, "Sub ek," it's all one. So what is the truth of "us" versus "them"? Here, Ram Dass helps us to understand what "us" versus "them" encompasses.

Some years ago I had an interesting dialogue with my father. This was back in the seventies and the commune days, and a group of us produced a six-record album of lectures and music and radio shows, called *Love Serve Remember.* It had a beautiful photographic book with stories in it. We distributed it for $4.50. Of course, the economy was different back then in the seventies, and it did very well.

My father looked at it and he said, "That's a very impressive piece of work." I said thank you, because he didn't always agree with most of what I was doing. He said, "You know, this thing is worth a lot more than $4.50. You probably could charge nine to ten dollars for this. Would the same number of people buy it?" I said, probably. He said, "I don't understand."

I said, "Well, it cost us $3.50 to produce and there is a profit in it of a dollar and that seems reasonable."

He said, "Are you against capitalism?"

I tried to figure out how I could talk to my father about this, and I said, "You're a lawyer. Last year you tried a case for Uncle Henry, didn't you? Was it a hard case?"

He said, "Damn right. I had to spend a lot of time at the law library."

I said, "Did you win?"

He said, "Yeah, I won."

I said, "You charge pretty good fees to your clients. I bet you charged him a healthy fee for that."

He said, "Don't be an idiot. It was Uncle Henry."

I said, "That's my problem. If you can find somebody who isn't Uncle Henry, I'll rip them off. If you can find somebody who's *them*, I will charge them whatever the market will be."

You see, I want to live in a world of *us*, not in a world of *them*.

Who Is *Us* and Who Is *Them*?

In order to play our roles, we are often required to define people as "us" and "them." This is very subtle. When we start out as tribes, the tribe is *us*. We run into another tribe and maybe we decide that because there's only one buffalo available, the other tribe becomes *them* because we have to protect the buffalo meat for our own tribe. So it's *us* against *them* and we share the buffalo among us and we compete against them.

In a competition paradigm in business, whom you're competing against is *them* and we in our company are *us*. But it doesn't stop there. If you're an administrator or an executive, you have to motivate the people in your company to get a certain level of productivity. To some extent, you are seeing your employees as *them* as well as trying to get the best out of them. You say nice things about *us*, but you're thinking *them*. So now your employees are *them*, and you are *us*, meaning the administration. Of course, you as an executive are surrounded by peers who are waiting for your misstep because they're trained in the same competitive school that you are. So at some level, your colleagues in your own company are a little bit *them* as well.

Well, you say, at least I've got my family; they're *us*. But now your husband or wife is very upset because you're spending so much time in business. They don't understand how important this is, and because they don't understand or appreciate your predicament, you start to think of your family as *them*. Then within the family, of course, there's the issue of generations. The kids don't understand. They're a different generation, so the kids are *them*. My parents don't understand, and they become *them*. You slowly are getting cut off from the generations.

So I am left with only me. I started out with us as the tribe, and now I've got us down to just me. One step further is when you start to think about yourself as an object. You become alienated even from yourself, and you have ultimate and total alienation.

Are "They" Evil?

I was on a program together with Al Hunt [a columnist for *Bloomberg View*] and he was talking about Jesse Helms [a conservative senator from North Carolina who opposed civil rights, homosexuality, and all liberal ideals]. Al didn't like Jesse Helms and he said that Jesse Helms *is an evil man*. I haven't said this to Al yet, but I'd like him to reconsider whether he'd be willing to say Jesse Helms *is a being who does evil acts*. That's a very critical distinction because the minute you identify somebody with their acts, when you find their acts reprehensible, you reject them.

There is a quote from the poet Kabir that says, "Do what you do with another human being, but never put them out of your heart." Never close your heart down to them. I watch in myself how hard that is to learn.

In the Reagan administration, I had considerable difficulty

with Caspar Weinberger, who served as secretary of defense under Reagan. I had difficulty with some of his policies, so I took a picture of Caspar and put it on my altar with all my holy pictures, along with Buddha and Christ. I'd say, "Good morning, Christ. Good morning, Buddha. Hello, Ramana Maharshi." Then I'd sort of moan, "Hello, Caspar." I could see how far away I was from being able to keep my heart open to this being, even though it was his acts I didn't like. It was like Gandhi saying, "The British must leave India, but I want them to leave as friends." I want to keep the *us* quality going even though in the game they must move out. That is really such an incredible art form in human relations—the ability to keep the quality of *us* going.

Of course, I am horrified by the actions of brutality, rape, and murder. But as I look at the faces of the Bosnian Serb cabinet, for example, at those people, at *them*, I see they are *us*. People don't feel heard. They don't feel heard by me and I can't hear them. I see how communication breaks down. I'm reminded of an interview I did with Zalman Schachter [the founder of the Jewish Renewal movement]. I said, "Zalman, if you were an Israeli, what would you say to an Arab?"

He said, "*Oy*. You know, before we can be together, we have to learn to grieve with one another."

We can no longer afford a *them*. Either *us* makes it or nobody makes it. And yet we are living with an anachronistic mythology that implies some people can still make it at the expense of others. We still think the *us* can become joyful without apologizing to the Native Americans. We still think that wealthy people can hold on to their IRAs in the midst of inner-city turmoil.

The Myth of the Individual

The fact is that the myths in our culture, which are so much based on individuality, have led us down a path that has isolated us very profoundly from each other. The myth of the individual succeeding on his own, doing whatever he needs to do and using whatever he needs to do it with, has become acceptable since the Industrial Revolution. As ecology becomes an issue, we're seeing that individual nations working alone is not acceptable; it's kind of a dysfunctional cosmology now, even if it wasn't before.

The myth of the individual developing their own strengths and capacities is a major trap because it ends up leaving a person (or a nation) caught in separateness. This is an interesting quality of separateness; it's separateness of the mind in which you are thinking about other people because you're identified with your own needs. The interesting thing about identification with your own needs and desires is that it colors everything in your world in terms of what you perceive others to be because you see them only in relationship to the satisfaction of that desire. Your motivation affects your perception. If you are hungry, you see what's edible. If your car is breaking down, you notice service stations. The minute you identify very strongly with a desire, you only see other people in relation to the gratification of that desire. In other words, you have made everybody around you into an object.

The cost of that is incredible. When you have a desire and you think about how to satisfy it, you think about somebody as an object to be manipulated. To bring about the gratification of your desire, you separate yourself from them, and what gets starved in that process is both you and them. This separation closes down the quality of the heart connection between human beings, which is an extremely painful cutting off.

Most of us don't have much control over this because our desires take us over. I've watched myself in the most horrible and ghastly situations. I can be sitting so loving and spacious and caring and open toward people and then, say, lust will enter into me as if it came from somewhere else. But it comes, it awakens, it arises, and suddenly my whole perceptual apparatus shifts. In the Hindu tradition, you'd say I went into my second chakra, into the plane where suddenly I see everybody in one of three categories—potentially makeable, a competitor, or irrelevant. I watch myself go from being this very open spiritual being to looking at everybody in this way. To my horror, I am ready to use everything and anything in the service of gratifying this desire.

When we have these powerful desires, like lust or the desire for power that comes out of inadequacy, out of fear, out of feelings of loneliness, we will manipulate the people around us in order to get what we want. In the process, we treat them as objects, not as *us*, but as *them*. Those of you who have been subject to feelings of lust know that the difference between lust and love is that lust manipulates an object for the gratification of your own desires. The minute that desire system is gratified, the other person is a literal stranger to you because you know them as an object. You've never let them in as a fellow being.

If I develop my identity as a teacher, I need you as an audience or students in order to legitimize my definition of myself.

So I'm constantly looking to you. I'm manipulating you to get you to give me back something I need to reassure me that I am who I think I am. The identification with my own separateness starts to make me use everybody around me to get that.

You can feel that in your own lives again and again and again. If you feel yourself to be a competent mother, you need your children to be a certain way to legitimize your role as a mother. The minute you need somebody else to fulfill a model you have of yourself, you start to manipulate the other person. Don't think the other person doesn't feel manipulated. They do. And then you're dealing with an interesting situation in which you are creating paranoia in other people who feel that they are being used and exploited.

The problem we're facing is that most of us create models about how we think life ought to be. Like the woman who thinks that to be a good mother, her children must be a certain way. My mother felt that her children should be clean and neat and quiet, seen and not heard. Every time we were heard as well as seen, or every time we were dirty, we were a threat to her definition of herself. As much as she loved us, what she loved us as was her children, not as us. She didn't hear *me*. She only needed me to be what she needed me to be in order to feel adequate because she felt very insecure as a human being.

You can see how you do this in interpersonal relationships—using people to fulfill your needs or your models or your expectations. If you really loved me, you would be whom I need you to be in order for me to feel that I'm okay. That's a very convoluted process, and it's the process that most of us are living with most of the time.

What Makes Us *Us*?

There's plenty that makes you and me *them* to each other. Some are men, some are women, some old, some young, some from Europe, some from Africa, but look at the things that are *us*. There are qualities that bring us together. Where do we focus on the *us* and where do we focus on the *them*? Oh, okay, it's you who are the one that tells the old fishing story. You are the one who puts the garbage out, and so on.

As long as you are identified with yourself as a separate entity, then you are always in relationship with others as objects. The minute you cultivate that part of you that is connected, that is part of the web of things in which we are *us*, then another quality comes into human relationships. You recognize the quality of love, of coming into love with people, because all of the ways in which we are separate are at some level rooted in fear. And one way of characterizing the dialogue of humanity is the dialogue between fear and love.

I was doing a benefit in Boulder for Earth Day and there was a mime act before me. They did a skit with a little sign that said *them* on the placard. They went through this thing of do you think *they* are watching? What'll *they* think if I pick my nose? It was a whole thing about *them* and how you grow up worrying about what will *they* think. What will *they* think if you wear shorts when you go out? What will people think? And they did it very well.

I was going on late, at 11:00 p.m., which is hardly the time to give a heavy lecture. You don't serve the roast beef at eleven, or the soy burger as the case may be. So I made a sign and it said *us*. I said, "Well, I know it took me five years of analysis, but I finally accepted that I'm *us*. I mean earlier I was *them*, too, but now I'm *us*. I obviously can accept the fact that you are *us* because you and I are here on Earth Day, which is good." Everybody said, "Yes, yes, we're all *us*." I said, "What about the shah of Iran? [Feel free to substitute any present-day leader.] Is the shah of Iran *us* or is he *them*? How about Ronald Reagan, *us* or *them*? Where do you want to draw your line? Now, if it's all *us*, it's quite a different trip than if it's *them*. If it's them, you better lock your door, get your .22. But if it's *us*, far out."

Aren't we complex, exquisitely interevolved organisms?

Two Planes of Consciousness

It's as if we have two clear, obvious mechanisms for being in the universe. One is through the mind that processes sense data and thoughts and relates to the world as object. The mind is continually setting boundaries. This is me, this is not me. This is good, this is bad. The mind is constantly judging. The battle goes on between what's *us* and what's *them*.

There is another way we can know one another beyond our minds—*through our intuitive hearts*. And then there's this other quality of the heart, like the expression "My heart goes out to you." The quality of the heart is it loves without discrimination. It just loves. It has no boundaries. This way of knowing one another is subtle. It is often hidden behind the more obvious ways of knowing through senses and thought. But if we know what to look for, and cultivate our intuitive way of knowing, we find out for ourselves that we are much more than body and personality. While no name is entirely satisfactory for this other dimension of ourselves, for the purpose of our discussion, the word "soul" will do.

The journey after getting high or becoming free is learning how to stand nowhere by not grabbing or standing against anything. You go through stages of sequential-ness where you get incredibly high and it's all one thing, then you get incredibly caught and it's all another thing, then you pull back awhile and you get incredibly high, and then the toxins sneak in and you get caught in your stuff and it's horrible, and then you go and meditate some more. . . .

Well, I guess that's what I've been doing for thirty-two years now, from the time the mushrooms catapulted me into another plane of consciousness—playing with the planes of consciousness. William James said, "Our normal waking consciousness . . . is but one special type of consciousness, whilst all about it, parted from it by the filmiest of screens, there lie potential forms of consciousness entirely different. We may go through life without suspecting their existence; but apply the requisite stimulus, and at a touch they are there in all their completeness."

All the maps from the East and my guru and all the practices started to teach me about these other planes, which are not planes at all because that's conceptual crap. You pick out what your karma demands. Everybody's creating it all the time. That's a dualistic plane, way up near the top, but it's like foreplay. Once you have started that journey of awakening and you realize that that plane is real and it's who you are and you start to yearn to be established in that plane of reality, you then start to look around for methods; all religious traditions are basically methods for moving you from your separateness into the experiential realm of oneness. On the street it's called "getting high" and everybody wants to get high, but the interesting thing is that high isn't free. High is just high, and high is part of the polarities of the world in which the opposite of high is low: you go up and you come down and you go up and you come down and you go up and you come down. You do it thousands of times.

Here's another plane. Paramahansa Yogananda asked the Indian saint Anandamayi Ma to tell him something of her life. She said:

> Father, there is little to tell. My consciousness has never associated itself with this temporary body. Before I came on this Earth, Father, I was the same. I grew into womanhood, but still I was the same. When the family in which I had been born made arrangements to have this body married, I was the same. And, Father, in front of you now, I am the same. Even afterwards, though the dance of creation changed around me in the hall of eternity, I shall be the same.

We focus so much on individual differences, our uniqueness, that to flip it around and say how we're all the same, then go into the place where we are the same now and then as well as here and there, is like when Mother Teresa is lifting a leper out of the gutter. For most people, that is an act of deep kindness. If you ask her what she is doing, she is ministering to her beloved Christ in all his disguises. Now you may be a leathery cynic and say, "Gee, she really bought the party line," but I think not. I think she beat the system.

The art form, as I see it, is to get down to moment by moment. Forget/remember until you are full out forgetting and remembering simultaneously. It's living life with passion *and* with total emptiness. Freedom is passionate delight in form and at the same moment total emptiness.

From the "Us" of the Sixties to the "Them" of Fundamentalism

Part of what was so exciting about the sixties was the undercutting of the vertical patriarchal institutional structures of society. There was an increasingly shared awareness that these kinds of monolithic institutions were like paper tigers, the creation of our collective mind. There was a moment when people surrounded the Pentagon and held hands and *om*ed to make it rise. Now, only some people saw it rise, but what a statement that was! The Pentagon, which seemed like such a real thing, was just this thing you made rise and fall. It trivialized the Pentagon in a way or put it back in perspective when it had been bigger than life.

When we got free in the sixties, then suddenly it was the empowering of the individual heart, the intuitive heart that said, "Hey, there's work to do in civil rights. There's work to do in sexual freedom. There's work to do with women's issues and gay and lesbian issues. There's work to do with our foreign policy and the anti–Vietnam War movement." There was a link between the intuitive heart of individuals and the feeling of rightness or appropriateness between that and these dissonant institutions that were out of line.

The problem was that those of us who had experienced that

quality of love had such a sense of the power of love that we underestimated the power of fear. Tim Leary and I had a chart on our wall at Millbrook, a geometrically rising curve showing how fast everybody would get enlightened. It did involve putting LSD in the water supply, but other than that it was not terribly dramatic. It seemed so inevitable and irrevocable because the experience was so powerful and so irreversible once it had happened that we started to surround ourselves with other people who had experienced it. Kennedy was in office and lots was happening in the Haight-Ashbury and the rock 'n' roll movement. Minstrels like Bob Dylan were carrying these messages of the relative nature of reality that undercut the power of any one point of reality. The carriers of Native American wisdom were our elders instead of objects of sadism.

What happened to us in the sixties was so strong that we assumed everybody would fall before it. But they didn't. There were the people who didn't have that experience. What they experienced was that the whole social structure in which they had power was under attack. They got frightened and they pushed against it. In that sense, the sixties polarized the culture because it was naive. It only understood its own perception and assumed its perception would spread by osmosis. I now see that the naivete with which we embraced our idealism fed the fundamentalist and right-wing movement in the United States.

I accept that I have as much responsibility as others do for creating what actually happened, which was a whole group of people who weren't part of the game, part of that experience of love, got frightened. In that sense, the sixties created a *revolutionary* rather than an *evolutionary* process in the culture, a pendulum swing. And, as a repercussion, we had fundamentalist conservatives building very, very tight, new vertical structures, so that at this moment we have between six hundred thousand and a million of us in jail.* That's the largest percentage of an imprisoned population of any country in the world.

What's interesting to me now is that there is a lot going on, there's a destabilizing, but we won't be so naive this time. We won't think that everybody will see that love conquers fear just because we saw it. I'm not going to get discouraged in the way the world game is falling, but we can't polarize again; we can't have an *us* and *them*. We've got to keep embracing people. Is it possible for us, as conscious and compassionate people, to push against the limit, define the limit, and at the same moment keep our hearts open to these beings?

An interesting nature of the dynamics of change in a social system is the ability to say no to somebody without closing your heart. The fundamentalist movement would probably punish somebody like me if it had its choice. I'm a threat to that system. I was working with an Alan Watts quote that basically said any unity that we arrive at through love or violence or coercion from outside won't work. The way in which we will come into an honoring of diversity is by recognizing our unity behind our diversity and then honoring our diversity. When we meet as beings, we can say, "Well, what is your unique way of expressing your dharma? What is your unique way of manifesting in the

* As of 2022, there were 1.9 million people incarcerated in the United States. https://www.prisonpolicy.org/profiles/US.html.

world to relieve suffering?" You may say, "Well, I really feel that the imminence of ecological environmental disaster is what demands my attention." Someone else says, "Look, I am from an indigenous people and we have wisdom to share with the world. You are not listening and we are going to demand you listen." I can honor both of those agendas.

The question is, Could we hear behind all of our agendas in order to hear that we are fellow human beings and then go from there out into our diversity? That's the issue we come to in all of the polarizations in the culture. I can get very scared by the idea of Islamic fundamentalism and jihad. I could feel the same thing with a Christian fundamentalist as with an Orthodox Jew. My job is to work on myself, so I experience the place at which we're us and then honor the diversity and the right of that person to do what they want. But when they start to do something that affects me or another person's rights, then I have to say no. Then I have to work to say no without closing my heart. That's the sequence I go through.

Chapter 2

From Judgment to Appreciation

We humans are a judgmental lot. We are constantly turning us *into* them *by saying* they *are too much this or too little that, basically so we can feel better about ourselves. But we are also separating internally into the good angel on one shoulder and the mean devil on the other, judging ourselves harshly for what we see as our personal failings. I'm too fat, too weak, too old, too tired. . . . Wait a minute while I beat myself up some more.*

Ram Dass always talked about the first lines of the Hsin Hsin Ming *by the Third Chinese Patriarch of Zen:*

> *The Great Way is not difficult for those who have no preferences. When love and hate are both absent, everything becomes clear and undisguised. Make the smallest distinction, however, and heaven and earth are set infinitely apart.*

But make distinctions we do. All the time.

Here, Ram Dass leads us from judgment to appreciation, and in so doing shows us how to bring heaven and earth together again.

I understand that my life experiences are the gift of my guru in order to bring me to God. If somebody upsets me, that's my problem. This is a hard one. We don't usually think this way in this culture, but I've learned to see other people like trees in the forest. It's interesting that when you go out into the woods and look at trees, you appreciate the trees. You appreciate an oak and an elm and a pine. A gnarled tree is a gnarled tree and a straight tree is a straight tree. If you're in the lumber business, it's different, but for most of us we're looking at a tree and enjoying the tree for itself, appreciating the tree, appreciating its uniqueness. You're not inclined to say, "I don't like you because you are a pine and not an elm." You appreciate trees the way they are, but the minute you look at humans, notice how quickly that changes.

When you come near humans, you go into your judging mode. You say better/worse, older/younger. Should be this, should be that. I'm better than she is or I'm better than you. I'm right. He shouldn't have done that. They're bad. There's a way in which you don't allow humans to manifest the way they are. I am very different from you, and you are all different from each other, and so on. The question is whether we climb into our differences or not, or whether we manifest our individuality through them.

You take whatever others do or say personally, but what they really are is mechanical runoff of old karma. They look real and they think they're real, but what they are is mechanical runoff. It's all conditioned stuff. If somebody comes along and gets to me, they get me angry or uptight or they awaken some desire in me, wow, I am delighted! They got me! And that's my work on myself. If I'm angry with you because your behavior doesn't fit my model of how I think you should be, that's my problem for having models. No expectations, no upset.

If you're a liar and a cheat, that's your karma. If I'm cheated, that's my work on myself. My attempting to change you, that's a whole other ball game. What I'm saying is I will only be happy if you are different from who you are. Think of how many relationships you say, "I really don't like that person's this . . . If they would only be that . . . If I could only manipulate them to be this, I could be happy." Isn't that weird? Why can't I be happy with them the way they are? You're a liar, a cheat, and a scoundrel, and I love you. I won't play any games with you, but I love you. It's interesting to move to the level where you can appreciate love instead of constantly bringing in that judging component, which is really rooted in your own feelings of lack of power.

The Discriminating Mind

A judgmental mind is usually motivated by fear. To get attached to preferences comes out of fear, which comes out of separateness. *Discriminating mind*, on the other hand, comes out of wisdom. "Discriminating" doesn't mean *discrimination* against the "other" based on race or religion or any other difference. It is more like the Vedic phrase *neti neti*, which means "not this, not that" or "neither this nor that." I think the discriminating mind is wonderful. You can see this is different from that. White is different from yellow is different from blue. A person whose attention is drawn toward awakening is different from somebody whose attention is drawn toward greed and lust, or personal gratification only. To see the difference between things is wisdom, the going beyond the two to the One.

When you move into some altered states of awareness, you see everything as equally acceptable as everything else. You go behind good and evil. You go behind the two and you see the One. You see nothing is any different from anything else. Nothing. Death, life, murder, joy, all of it. It's just all there. It's all phenomena. And then you come back into dualism, you come back into polarities, you come back into planes where there is a preference, a choice, a difference.

When you impose judgment upon the discrimination, it's like saying that spring, when the trees have buds on them, is better than fall, when the leaves are all red before they fall off. It's just a different stage in the cycle. We're all part of cycles. Understanding that these are parts of vast processes means it is nothing personal. You are part of all those tiny little fish you see down in the water that are leaping up and jumping across in the sunlight. At one level, we are busy thinking stuff, but like these tiny fish, we are just phenomena occurring, nothing better or worse. Is it better if the fish would jump a different way? They're just fish. We're just human.

Being Judged

The fear of being on the receiving end of judgment from others is ego, ego, ego. The ego is so entrenched in fear. The soul is entrenched in love. That feeling of *they are judging me* is a thought, and you don't want to identify with any thought. As Timothy Leary said, "I'm tired of being should upon." Turn your identification in your heart and say, "I am loving awareness," and then you will be aware of that thought. You'll see another thought, another thought, another thought. All ego, ego, ego.

Most of us have used other people's eyes to evaluate ourselves. I used to do it all the time. That's how I was climbing the ladder of academia. But now I don't. I see that other people's evaluation of me is their karma. It's not my business. They have their karma and it's not going to affect me.

Once I was lecturing in Chicago and I decided one afternoon to go to a pornographic movie called *Deep Throat*. I was standing in line at the box office with my five dollars, with about five people in front of me. Then, walking down the street was this young, beautiful guy who was obviously very spiritual and light. He came up to me as I was busy standing in line and his eye caught mine. He said, "Ram Dass?"

I found myself palming my five-dollar bill. I realized I was the last one in line. I could say to him, "Yeah, hi, you walking this way?" I could keep walking and then I could go around the block and come back and hit the movie later. I saw his eyes go from me down the row to the box office, up to the marquee and back, and I could see his eyes were like cash registers or like a pinball machine or a one-arm bandit going through oranges, bananas, cherries. It was blowing his mind that who he thought I was could be standing in front of a pornographic movie.

The line moved forward at that moment and I had a choice. I said to him, "Excuse me, I'm in line." And I lost him at that moment, to the extent he wanted what I was supposed to be. Great tantric teaching. Actually, I just wanted to see the movie.

The mind is constantly judging, which clouds your ability to see *what is* and leads to preferences. You prefer this over that. Ram Dass the spiritual teacher, not Ram Dass the porno moviegoer, down to the root of preferring life over death. Judging things takes you away from life until finally you see that this leads to this or that leads to that, and you understand how it all works.

The problem about judging is where you're standing in relation to it. When you are in a place with another person where you are sharing how you see the universe, you are not the judge. You are merely sharing discriminative wisdom as you see it and you're sharing it with them as *us*. The judging that I'm talking about is where *I judge you*, and that's a different and very delicate issue in a relationship.

Very often the contract between two people isn't for truth. The contract is "You don't bug my ego, I won't bug yours." When people say, "Let us seek for truth," the way in which you give truth to another human being is very dependent upon where your own consciousness is. You can give truth to another person, even very harsh truth, that brings you two closer together, or you can bring truth to them in a way which is very divisive. It's where you are in relation to the information. It's the judge that we're dealing with. It's that identification with judging, not with discrimination between this and that.

As you quiet inside, you notice your own thoughts a little more clearly. You will see your father's voice and your mother's voice and all the voices of your education inside your head constantly saying things to you. Freud called it the "superego."

You'll see that the judge is inside and you keep giving it power by identifying with it. You feel yourself at war with the part of you that's doing it. Then there's a part of you that's judging what you're doing.

As a psychologist, I could study these phenomena in another person. Why not study it in myself? Part of what drugs did for me, and then meditation and all the spiritual things did for me, is help me stand back and get outside of it to see it for what it is . . . just stuff. Phenomena, phenomena. When you look at yourself as a set of phenomena, what is to judge? Is that flower less beautiful than this one? It's different. You begin to appreciate your uniqueness without it being better or worse. Cultivating an appreciation of uniqueness rather than preferences is very good. Don't confuse uniqueness and specialness. We want to be special when we don't feel we're enough, when we are what we are. Listen and hear what your unique manifestation is.

Self-Judgment

The fierceness of the judgment we have about ourselves is so unrelenting, rather than looking at ourselves and saying, "I am what I am, and this is it. It's like a pine tree or an oak tree or a river or a stone. I am it. My humanity is part of what I am. Despite all the trainings and shoulds that were laid upon me, I am what I am." But the minute I think I am not enough or I feel I'm in a vulnerable position, I will be inclined to use everything in my environment to secure my position. I will often judge things in ways to make myself feel more secure. I will also use judging in order to reinforce that deep place in myself where I feel strange or insecure.

I remember when I was feeling full of Dick Alpert inadequacies—Dick Alpert doesn't even feel he has a right to exist on earth; his whole life is an apology—and Dick is sitting in front of Maharajji and Maharajji is saying, "Go back to America." This is 1972 and I'd already been a so-called spiritual teacher for a couple of years in the West. Everywhere I went it was "Hello, Ram Dass, lead us." What was I going to do? I said, "Maharajji, you can't send me back. I'm too impure."

He looked at me, squinted, and he came up close and he looked in my ears and he looked very quizzical. Finally he said, "I don't see any impurities." I thought, Oh God, what is he doing? He can't mean it. I wouldn't let go. I just wouldn't let go of my little place in the dark.

The judging mind is always pulling something up or putting something down. For example, people on the spiritual path often have this subtle judging quality about others as to whether or not they are more conscious or more spiritual or more evolved. That's like looking at somebody who's thirty years old and saying they are better than somebody who's fifteen. What kind of nonsense is that? You can say, "Well, that one's thirty and that one's fifteen. It isn't better or worse; it's just different." And that's the same with spiritual awakening. It isn't an achievement; it is a matter of evolution. The beginning of awakening and the end of awakening are just different stages of the wheel, so don't get so judgmental.

Part of what Maharajji did for me was knowing everything in my mind and heart so deeply. He showed me many times that he knew what was in my mind—all those things you couldn't conceivably let another human being know because it would put you in such a vulnerable and embarrassing position. These thoughts were pouring through my head as I sat in front of him one day with my eyes closed while he talked to other people. I finally opened my eyes and there he was, about this far from my head. He was looking at me with a quality of such love that I could see my behavior wasn't necessary to his existence. He was resting in his own being; he didn't need my love or my goodness to make it all right. He didn't need anything from me. He looked at me the same way he would look at the stars or at a tiger eating a deer. He could look at the universe without judgment and I could be just what I am.

It started a process in me, which has gone on over the years. What happens for many of us who took drugs or had very profound experiences is it takes years to grow into what happened. It's taken me twenty-five years to grow into some of the things that happened to me on my first acid trip and what happened to me with Maharajji. I'm still in awe. But finally something let go in me and I opened and experienced a little deeper quality of my own beauty. I started to accept that I am okay just as I am, and that there is beauty in my being. I look at other people and I can hardly bear how beautiful you all are to me, even the ones who are busy being as unbeautiful as they can be because they think they are so unbeautiful. As judging as they can be, and even judging of me, I look and see such incredible beauty.

I'm Right; You're Wrong

Maharajji was always teaching me not to be arrogant about what I believed, not to feel righteous about feeling like I was right in my judgment of a situation or person. There were times when I thought myself to be right and stubbornly clung to that belief, although I had judged wrong.

In 1969, I was up in New Hampshire, at my father's farm, hiding out in a cabin, living like I had lived in India. I got a call from a young fellow from New York who wanted to come up and see me. His father had been a Russian scientist who had defected to the West; they were a relatively wealthy family. He had left the family and was living on the Lower East Side of New York with his girlfriend.

He came up to see me and we sat together. He was an extraordinary guy, a very pure being. He wanted to do hatha yoga, and he wanted to study with me. I had been studying it for some years, so I taught him some things. He was going to stay at his parents' island on a nearby lake, and he was going to come over and see me every week. But something happened before he left that day which shook me quite a bit. We were sitting and looking into each other's eyes, when suddenly a very powerful flash of light, like a lightning bolt, occurred between our third eyes. It was so violent that both of us fell over backward, stronger than either of us were. There wasn't any question of whether it had happened to both of us because we were both completely shocked by it. I didn't understand it. He went away.

He started coming back every week, and by the end of the summer, he was a more advanced yogi than I was, which didn't take much. I said, "Now you need a real teacher. I've taken you as far as I can. I can suggest some good hatha yogis."

He said, "No, I'm going into a cave on my parents' ranch in Arizona for the winter. If I can, I'll fly to wherever you are once a month and see you. I am going to do fasting and I'm going to live alone and see what happens." He did that and every month he'd come and see me wherever I was on the road. He began to look more and more like a yogi. He was very thin and very clear. He was doing many hours of meditation, fasting nine days at a time. He was living alone, an extraordinarily clear guy.

March came along and he didn't show up. In the middle of April, I got a letter from his mother that said, "My son entered *mahasamadhi*." It means "the great samadhi." It means he died, but he died into enlightenment, which is a strange thing for a mother to say, by the way. I immediately distrusted it because no student of mine's going to get enlightened. I mean, I'm not enlightened. She came a few weeks later and showed me his diary. On the last pages he had written, "Dear Mother, I have finished my work. Tell Ram Dass I am done. I am with Christ and Maharajji. I will look over you always. You need to have no fear for yourself or for me. Vaya con Dios," and he signed his name. She said, "You see, he finished. Don't you think so?"

Well, now, I'll tell you what I thought, truthfully. The writing was big and scrawly, just a few words on each page. I looked at it and thought, Where have I seen that before? Then I remembered when I used to take LSD, and in the middle of a session, when you're out at the farthest point, when you can't recognize your hand as a hand, you find something that is the greatest wisdom you've ever touched in the universe. It might be a word that unravels all the mysteries of the universe, so you better write it down for later. You stagger across the floor and grab a pen and write the word, which may turn out to be "be" or "is" or something. The next day it looks just like "be" or "is," but at that moment, from where you were sitting, it meant everything. I saw that kind of scrawly word and I thought, Uh-oh, it looks to me like he took acid and he died from maybe doing hatha yoga while on acid. He didn't have control, and it's really not enlightenment. So I said, "Well, I don't really know, but I know somebody who does know. I'll tell you what, why don't you send me a picture of him and I'll take it to Maharajji when I go to India next year, and I'll ask him. Because he'll know."

She sent me her son's high school graduation picture, which looked just like any other high school graduation picture. I put it in my suitcase for going to India. Two weeks later, his brother comes to visit me. His brother says, "I've got to confess to somebody. I went to visit my brother with a friend of mine. We all took acid together and went swimming. My brother was in a very high state. He came over to me and he went to embrace me and I went into a homosexual panic and pushed him away. He got paranoid and told us to leave and we left. That was the last I ever saw him alive."

I thought, *Aha!* He took acid, he got paranoid, he went back to his cave. He did hatha yoga to try to get over it and he did himself in, clearly. Ego, ego, ego, no enlightenment, zero. Send him around again, Charlie.

When I got back to India, I didn't find Maharajji for a long time because he's very elusive. Finally we did find him, and one day, four or five of us were sitting around his takhat [wooden platform]. He was going into people's bags like a monkey and opening them up and throwing stuff and looking at pictures. It was all this kind of love play. Suddenly I remembered this high school picture I had in my bag. I'd completely forgotten about it. I got the picture and I put it on his bed in front of him. Maharajji was playing and laughing and talking. I didn't say a word, I just put it there.

He looked at it for a second, looked at me, and said, "He's dead." Pretty good, from a high school picture. I said, "Yes." Then he said, "He completed his work. He is one with Christ. His mother should not worry. He is watching over her. He loves you very much, Ram Dass. He doesn't want you to worry about him. He's finished his work." Quoting word for word from the boy's diary.

Then he said to me, "He died from your medicine," meaning LSD. I said, "I knew it!" And he said, "*Nay!* He finished his work."

At that moment, what happened was two parts of my mind came together. In my mind, you couldn't die from acid and be enlightened, but he was saying that when you finished your work, whatever the way you leave isn't the big issue. When you're done, you go. He had, in fact, done what he needed to do, and that was merely his exit routine. That was the way the hook came out on the stage, time to leave.

And time for me to leave judgment behind.

Righteousness

I examine self-righteousness in myself, of which I have a large dollop because I am really so good I can hardly bear it. I am really good. It is really nauseating. I see that it's because of a deep-rooted sense of feeling that I'm not good enough, that I don't have a right to exist, that I have to constantly take a stance to prove that I'm good, that I'm righteous.

I see the psychodynamic nature of righteousness. I also see the way in which it is a thought form, and as my meditative practice deepens and my mindfulness gets stronger, I see that quality of using situations to prove I'm good or good enough or that I'm right. I see the judging mind come up, which has in it that quality of righteousness or unrighteousness, and instead of climbing into it, I am mindful of its presence and then keep coming back into my awareness so that I am not as obnoxiously self-righteous as I used to be.

I think you become aware how using situations to prove things about yourself is not a very deep, nurturing quality for yourself. It's not a very interesting plane to end up working on all the time, and it cuts you off from people because you're constantly in a judging mode, constantly in the world of objects, of "Am I good enough? Are they good enough? Am I better than they are? Who's the best?" All of that sort of thing. And that ends up isolating you as somebody who is constantly in an alien or hostile world; you're constantly proving you're adequate and good enough and so on.

You've got to forgive everybody. Not forgiving keeps you from God. It locks you in a place of dense unforgiving righteousness. You're caught with pride, which makes you want to justify the position you've just been stuck in. That's righteousness. That's holding on to the place of "I'm right," which is pride. The other part of you wants to get on with it, and you just want to let go. If you let go, the ego gets battered. If you hold on to the ego, the living spirit gets battered and you end up righteous, but out of the spirit. Or you can end up forgiving, even though you were right, and you end up in the spirit again.

Anger usually is intimately related to righteousness. You'll notice that when you get angry at somebody, it is because you feel you have been wronged and you have a sense of right. It is said in the spiritual literature that righteousness, and being right, is one of the last gates to the inner temple. It's one of the last obstacles to getting in the inner temple.

One of the problems of spiritual work is ending up being a good yogi. You are a really good yogi. You do all the positions perfectly and you are really righteous and good, but you're not free. It's called the "golden chain," the chain of righteousness. You certainly see that in most religious traditions: the priest class gets very caught in being right. But freedom lies beyond good and evil. It lies beyond right and wrong. It goes beyond all polarities. When you want to become free, then your righteousness and your anger are much less interesting than they used to be. You feel less comfortable sitting in your righteousness than you do in throwing it back into the pot in order to become free.

Love Everyone and Tell the Truth

During my second trip to India, when other Westerners were there as well, Maharajji called me up and said, "Ram Dass, love everyone."

I said, "Yes, Maharajji." But, oh boy, the truth was I didn't love everyone.

I got called up two days running and he leaned way down, held my beard, and said, "Ram Dass, tell the truth."

Of course I said, "Yes, Maharajji." So I was left that day with what a liar I was. Each day he'd alternate between "love everyone" and "tell the truth." The peculiar predicament I found myself in was that he was giving me two contradictory instructions. The truth was I didn't love everyone.

So I thought maybe it'd be good to try telling the truth.

That'll be refreshing. And as I looked at all my gurubhai, my guru brothers, I realized I hated them all. They all took me away from him. I had spilled the beans about him in the first place with *Be Here Now* and now there were all these unworthy people hanging around, taking up Maharajji's time. I mean, they were nice enough people, but generally I'd find reasons to hate each one. The truth was I didn't like anybody. I even had a sign on my door that said "Do Not Enter."

At the same time, Maharajji had told me not to touch money. I now interpret that to mean I shouldn't cling to or fixate on money, but in those days I took it literally: I shouldn't touch money. So one of the group would be my bag person and carry my money. When we'd get on the bus to go to Kainchi, they'd pay my bus fare, which worked out fine until I got to hate them all. One day everybody got on the bus, and since I wasn't speaking to anyone, I had no money to get on the bus, so I had to walk all the way to the temple. They got there in about half an hour and it took me about three hours to get to the temple through the back woods. As I walked, I was getting more and more angry. I was furious.

When I came over the last hill and looked down on the temple, I saw all the Westerners laughing and hanging around Maharajji. He had obviously spent much more time with them than on any other day. I was full of loathing and hatred and hated myself and felt so impure even walking into the temple. As I came over, they were all eating their lunches. One of the people whom I especially despised came up with a leaf plate of food and offered it to me. I took it and threw it at him, which was very satisfying, very satisfying.

I remember the moment very clearly. I heard Maharajji

calling me from across the courtyard and I looked over at him and at that moment I hated him too. I was *really* angry. I sat down in front of him. He looked at me and said, "Something troubling you?"

I said, "Yeah. I hate all of them. They're mean; they're impure. And I hate myself."

He said, "Do you love me?"

I looked at him and fell apart. I started to sob, absolutely sob. I said, "I love you."

He sent for milk and he was pouring milk down my throat and he was patting me on the head and I went through this whole catharsis. Then he leaned over the takhat and we were nose to nose. He said, "I told you to love everyone."

I said, "But you told me to tell the truth. And the truth is I don't love everyone."

He said, "Ram Dass, love everyone and tell the truth."

At that moment, I experienced two things. First, I experienced a coffin in front of me and who I thought I was in that coffin. I thought I was somebody whose truth was that they didn't love everyone. He was describing who I would be when I finished being who I thought I was. Can you hear that?

The other thing was that, at that moment, I turned and looked over at my guru sisters and brothers and I saw that at one level I had all this righteous indignation about them, but one little flip of consciousness and I saw how incredibly beautiful each one of them was and I loved them so deeply. And that was the teaching. When I don't feel that love for another human being, I hear Maharajji saying, "Ram Dass, love everyone and tell the truth."

What my guru was saying to me was "Become free, let go."

He wasn't saying "Work it out." When I was angry at all those people at the temple, I was right about every one of them. They were irresponsible, sloppy. I had a reason for every one of the thirty-four people that I was angry at. And he said to me, "Let go. Love everyone and tell the truth."

What he was saying to me was "When you finish standing where you think you are, in which case those two instructions don't go together, you will end up standing in a place where they do go together, where the truth is you do love everyone." That was incomprehensible to me. I hated all these people, but as I looked at them with his words in my heart and mind, I saw that I hated their actions. But right behind that, if I shifted my gaze just a little bit, they were all souls caught in their own stuff, which led to their fears, which led them to do whatever they did. And that led me to judgment, while right behind it were these beautiful, pristine souls that I loved very dearly. So I flicked my gaze and I saw that I loved them.

Every time I held on to anger, even if I was right, I ended up cutting myself off. I had lived for years and years with a heart that was closed and tight and cut off, and I could feel how it affected everything in my life. What I then realized was that it was too painful to be right, that it was costing me more than it was worth and that I wanted to be part of the flow of the universe rather than to be sitting in judgment of it. Anger was not going to get me to God. It was hard because there was pride involved. I was right. And he didn't say, "Work it out." He said, "Give it up." I realized that went counter to my whole psychological training, but I decided that I wanted to be free. I don't have to sit in judgment; I don't have to play God with everybody around me. My job is to keep my heart open.

The Soul's Curriculum

There's a certain point at which the whole responsibility shifts. When you look at a soul coming into life with a curriculum that involves other people doing things to it, you realize that the soul is using the other person to do it to itself. This is a very tricky issue. For example, those of you that have problems with parents, one of the things is appreciating exactly what they were caught in and how they ended up being what they are.

Anger is only useful when it is rooted in love and equanimity, when the anger is an intentional emotional response that you use as a teaching device out of your love and equanimity. Like in Tibetan Buddhism, there are stories of a guru who keeps beating the student and being very angry and irritable. Actually, that wasn't the guru at all. That was a functional behavior that came out of love and wanting to liberate the other person. There was no hatred in it. That anger came out of compassion. But that's very rare.

When you look at somebody and say, "You did that to me," when you stand back a moment, they didn't do it to you. They did it because that's who they are. From a soul's point of view, the soul is creating the curriculum. In that sense, when your parent abused you, they were just doing what they were doing because they were out of control because of their desire systems, which are the result of their parents and on and on. From a soul's point of view, you were using them to do that to you because that's what you needed in your curriculum. Now, that's a heavy-duty spiritual interpretation. It doesn't mean it's a justification for not helping anybody or stopping something harmful. At the same moment, it is a way of looking at the people that have been involved in your life so that you can finally get free of judging your parents and judging the people around you. They didn't love me, they hurt me, he left me. All that stuff.

You begin to appreciate that, especially in relationships, you already knew the handwriting on the wall; you knew how it was going to come out. You've seen it in your friends: somebody gets out of a very destructive relationship and then you watch them get into another one that's going to be equally destructive. They're in the "Oh, it's so beautiful" stage and "This'll be altogether different," when they're doing the exact same thing. From the soul's point of view, you get to appreciate that each person is living out their drama and then they're interacting, and those interactions are the grist for each other's mill of awakening. From a personality point of view, you develop judgment. From a soul point of view, you develop appreciation.

Appreciate, Don't Judge

I've come to see that whenever you notice yourself judging, a beautiful practice is to flip it into appreciation. I still get lost a lot, but I've trained myself so that now a good percentage of the time I can feel the heaviness of the place that judging comes from. The minute I feel that, instead of "Oh shit, I'm judging," I immediately turn around and take that same thing and appreciate it.

I look at you just the way you are, and you're fine. You may think, Oh, if I lost twenty pounds . . . or As soon as I finish with a therapist next year . . . But you're fine. You're as fine as the trees outside. They're not busy saying, "Am I making it?" You with the mind, you with your prefrontal lobes, are you happier than the tree? No. It's interesting. You are out in the woods and you see pine trees and you say, "Ah, pine." Then you see a gnarled tree. "Ah, gnarled tree." But the minute you get around humans, it's not "Ah, slowpoke. Ah, essence of slowpoke. Wow. I haven't seen that in a long time." It's "Damn slowpoke." It's far-out—the shift to being an appreciator of life. It's not a big deal. You don't have to sign up for anything. It's just a flick of consciousness.

Part of the ability to be with other human beings is the ability to shift into appreciation rather than judging, to look at another human being—your child, your colleague, your employee—and appreciate their human predicament. I want to keep the *us* quality going even as we dance. Appreciation is really such an incredible art form in human relations.

The process is very much focused on finding that part of your mind from which you can watch the judging mind. The witness and the judging mind are different things. Noticing is different from judging. I can notice that I have too much fat in my middle and that my body is out of condition. I can notice that if I climb into feeling inadequate because of it or feel bad or react with remorse, guilt, shame, embarrassment, that's the whole quality of judging. But I can discriminate. I can see the difference between an iron body and a soft belly.

Most of the time when people are using the witness, it isn't really a higher faculty. It's mainly using a part of the intellect to observe the rest of your being. It's not vertical; it's a horizontal separation. Only later on do you develop a dispassionate separateness, which is not pushing away. It's from another level in which you have an intuitive sense of what's going on. That's a different level of the witness that comes for very few and it only comes later on. Don't get upset. It's all right. The witness is a good vehicle for getting distance. You've got to be careful that it doesn't have a judgmental quality to it and it doesn't involve closing the heart. The predicament is that a lot of times people use the witness as a way of defending against stuff.

It takes a long time to get out of looking at your uniqueness and judging it versus noticing it. If you substitute *noticing* for *judging*, you'll start to breathe a great sigh of relief. As long as you're in the judging mind, you're always separate from the world. You're separate from everything. I've really learned how to listen to hear what the contract is, listen to hear what people are asking, and then I notice that what burns me out is my frustration because everybody isn't in the same delusional system I am. Since I have no idea how my psychosis fits with this, all I can do is allow all of us to be crazy in our own ways. It's much more spacious and loving since I have come to understand that one truth. How can you do anything but appreciate that and love them so much that, if they're ready to change, they will change? I'm really less interested in changing other people than in changing myself and then being an environment in which other people change if they want to change, which doesn't sound like a strong social-activist position, but it may be the optimum one.

Chapter 3

Clinging/Attachment

Ah, attachment. We cling to pleasure and don't like pain. We cling to praise and try to avoid blame and criticism. We cling to name and fame and seek to avoid disgrace. We are attached to getting what we want, when and how we want it. We avoid losing at all costs. We cling to our thoughts and hold tight to our beliefs. We embrace those who agree with us and disparage those who can't see that we're right.

Every polarity finds us on one end of the spectrum or the other. Can I both love and hate you? Am I filled with faith or doubt? Does my personal balance sheet land on either loss or gain? Every position we cling to, every thought or emotion we are attached to, creates suffering, something about which the Buddha had a lot to say. As does Ram Dass.

I'm standing in a supermarket and I'm late and I'm tired and I've got a basket of groceries. A woman at the front of the line has a huge cart full of groceries. After it's all rung up and the clerk tells her how much it is, then the woman starts to open her pocketbook to find her checkbook and fill out the check and fill out the other part of the checkbook as well, and then get her identification, which she can't find. At some moment, I feel those mala beads in my fingers. Boy oh boy, did I get caught! Central casting really sent over a good one this time. Send him the woman with a checkbook, that'll get him. You begin to absolutely love the people that get you because they're showing you your secret stash of clinging, which you'd be inclined to overlook in your zeal to be enlightened.

There was a way in which I was frightened of city life, of the marketplace. I wanted to stay in the cave. I began to really hear the Buddhist teachings about the Four Noble Truths. The first one is the truth of suffering—birth, death, sickness, old age, more and more suffering every which way you look. The second Noble Truth is the cause of suffering. For an individual, that is the way the mind clings, the way awareness clings to something with attraction or aversion. You try to stop the process but everything's changing all the time. You're trying to freeze something, to hold it, hold on to your anger, hold on to whatever the experience is.

The third Noble Truth is you let go of the clinging of mind, pull the awareness back from thought and sense, and you're free. You're free of suffering. You have sensations and pain and phenomena, but you're not caught in suffering because you're not holding. And the fourth Noble Truth is the eightfold path of how to do it according to the Buddhist practices.

When Buddha looked for the root of all of that suffering, he saw that the basic root of suffering was the way the mind worked, the way we lost our connection to the wisdom that is nonconceptual, which is the root of our being from which actions spring. It's like the first line of the *Hsin Hsin Ming* by the Third Chinese Patriarch of Zen, which says the Great Way, meaning the deepest truth of things, is not difficult for those who have no preferences. The second line says, "When love and hate are both absent, everything becomes clear and undisguised." If you want to see the truth of things, then hold no opinions for or against anything. Now that bugged me. I mean, how can you live when you have no opinions? After all, I come from a family of lawyers. I figured out that the art is to have opinions and not have opinions at the same time. It comes out of the mystic line "One does nothing and nothing is left undone."

It's referring to two planes of consciousness. There's a plane where you're active and a plane where you're at rest. You're part of it all. What I saw was my aversion to form. I was trying to get high by pushing away that which brought me down. And I saw from the Buddhist point of view that as long as I had that aversion, as long as I was pushing anything away, it had me. Somehow I had to digest into myself the physical-psychological nature plane because if I pushed it away to get high, I wasn't free, and the game was to be free, not to be high. Finally I began to see that I had to integrate all these planes so I'm both high and low.

Nowhere to Stand

I heard the wisdom of the spiritual saying "There's nowhere to stand." That's a far-out line. Usually you think that way if you're stuck in psychological melodrama and you get out, so that you see it all with the witnessing eye of equanimity and clarity and nonattachment, then that's the place to stand. But that place is very passionless. If you are standing there in the witness and not experiencing the passions of life, then you're not experiencing your curriculum of incarnation, the breaking of the heart again and again. What's happening is you're still dealing with aversion and attraction.

I experienced it with my guru. I pegged him as this incredibly wise being who knew everything. He certainly knew hundreds of things about me. There was nowhere to hide. Once an old friend, a professor from Canada, came to visit me at the temple, and I thought I'd show off my guru to him.

Maharajji looked at him and he said, "Ah, you're from the United States."

The guy says, "No, I'm from Canada."

"You have five brothers and sisters."

"No," the man said, "I'm an only child."

I was slowly climbing under a rock. What's going on here? My guru's got everything wrong. Holy mackerel, have I picked the wrong guru?

The guy got up to leave, and as we were walking out, he said, "You've got a very nice guru," and he went away. I walked back into the ashram and there was Maharajji giggling away, telling me this guy's whole life story. Only he knows what that was all about.

I really began to see that there was nowhere to stand. Then I began to see that what was keeping me from being free was the clinging of my mind. Some of the clingings were to attractions and some of the clingings were to aversions. When I was in the state of seeing the oneness of all things, those attractions and aversions seemed just like the drama of it all. They were like all my neuroses. I had gone through drugs, analysis, gurus, yoga, you name it. I was a professor of neurosis at Harvard, yet I hadn't gotten rid of one neurosis with all those methods. Can you imagine? And I was an analyst. When I got into this oneness, all these neuroses, instead of these monsters that were coming down at me like beings from other planets to consume me, they were like little schmoozes.

Once you have begun to awaken, you can't fall off the path. There's no way. Where are you going to fall to? You going to make believe it never happened? You can forget for a moment, but it's in there. It's going to keep coming back and getting you and getting you. So don't get upset. It's okay. Go be worldly. Very often I push people into worldliness—go out, have more sex, more dope. Come on, make more money. Do it, do it. Do it until you're done with it.

Emmanuel

I had an interesting experience. I had been with this spook friend of mine, a disembodied being named Emmanuel. It's funny about these beings that aren't embodied. I have so many friends that are very liberal and they're not prejudiced. I mean, they're really not prejudiced. They're very open people. I could say to them, "I want you to meet a friend of mine." They'd say,

"Oh, of course." They wouldn't care if my friend was weird. But when I introduce them to a friend who has no body, some of them say, "Well, I don't know about that." Isn't that amazing? I mean, it's lurking prejudice.

It's tricky because you don't know whether the message is off-the-wall or profound. A real loser on this plane dies and then sends messages back like "Buy IBM" or something like that. Oh my God, yes. It came from a disembodied being. Well, a lot of disembodied beings are schlock jerks just like we are, so you've got to really listen to your disembodied beings with the same discrimination you do with embodied beings. But Emmanuel, he's cool. He's fun to hang out with.

Emmanuel speaks through a woman named Pat Rodegast. She doesn't disappear in the presence of Emmanuel; she's right there. It's more of a friendship, not a possession. I first heard Emmanuel on WBAI in New York, and you very rarely hear a disembodied being on the radio. He made such sense and was so charming and so light and so cosmic that I couldn't resist going to visit Pat and asking her to call upon him. I experienced Emmanuel as a definitely discreet separate entity with a distinct personality who is a dear friend of Pat's and who is like an uncle to me. I didn't experience Emmanuel as a free being but as a being in a different space in the universe of consciousness than I was. He had perspectives about life that I didn't have, which showed me where I was caught. So he was a useful teacher for me.

I said, "Emmanuel, what do I tell people about dying?"

He said, "Ram Dass, tell them it's absolutely safe." That's one of the best one-liners I've ever heard. Then he added, "Death is like taking off a tight shoe." And he knows because he remembers doing it. We did it, but most of us don't remember.

At one point I was talking to him about the moment of enlightenment and losing your separateness. He said, "You humans, with your dualistic minds." I thought, That's far-out. And he said, "Ram Dass, you're in school. Why don't you try taking the curriculum? Why do you treat your incarnation as if it was an error? Haven't you considered the possibility that you are in the right place at the right moment for what it is you need to learn?"

I said, "You mean . . . ?"

He said, "Yeah, you're a human being this time around. Why don't you try being human?"

See, I had never thought of that. That's like those experiments where they have a glass wall that's semicircular and they put an animal there and put its food behind the glass wall. In order to get the food, the animal has to go away from the food to go around the glass. Certain animals can't do it. They can never walk away from the food, so they never get around; they just keep beating their noses against the glass and starving. The pellet for me was divinity, and I was going for divinity. Somehow the idea that I'd go back into humanity to get to divinity . . . I just wasn't a high enough species to consider that possibility. But Emmanuel suggested it, and Alan Watts suggested it when he told me I was too attached to emptiness. It became obvious that that's where my path lay. I was pushing away my humanity, so I decided to become friends with my humanity. I thought, Why not?

I started to look at my life as my curriculum, and that got me fascinated with the uniqueness of my karmic predicament as a separate entity. I was busy not being separate all the time, but I realized that in order to be free of clinging to my separateness, I have to make peace with it. I have to be in harmony with it so I am neither separate nor not separate. I looked around and I saw different things that are places that I haven't cooked yet, that I haven't done much work with. I realized that to be fully in my incarnation meant to honor different parts of it that I had pushed out of the way.

Incarnation

Now I'm listening my way into my incarnation. What I have learned about suffering is that it's one thing to understand that your own suffering is due to the clinging of mind. It's really a whole other game with somebody else's suffering. As my guru said, "God comes to the hungry in the form of food," not in the form of spiritual dialogue or instruction. So at some point I felt pulled into tuning in to my incarnation, tuning in and honoring the different parts of it by being as impeccable as I can be.

What I've seen is my sequence of going from awakening (but not enlightenment) to renunciation in order to get high, to realizing that I wasn't free, to turning around to look at the physical plane that I had been busy pushing away. I realized there was nowhere to stand. I couldn't stand in heaven and look at earth so it wouldn't hurt. I realized I had to be able to dwell in the place where it hurts and it doesn't hurt—a perspective that would allow me to keep my heart open in hell. Even as my human heart was breaking again and again and again, my other heart, the one heart, the loving presence, always is.

When I turned around and stopped pushing away earth to get to heaven, I looked at this vast sea of suffering and this vast sea of beauty, because it's God made manifest in all these forms. It's full of awe: awesome, awful. And it's so intense. Each moment is so intense because each moment is full of all of it. It is a fully living moment. It's a whole other way of being in the moment. It hasn't built its house upon the sands of aversion and attraction. It's just looking at what is.

I had never thought about trying to be human as a way to get free. That seemed absurd and yet there it was. If I just turned around and embraced my humanity and stayed conscious, then I would hear the deep mystic teaching. Of course, you have to be nobody because somebody always stands somewhere. Once you realize that, you go into nobody training in order to extricate yourself from your attachment to your somebody-ness. Once you're nobody, then you can play Don Juan and you can huff and puff and make believe it matters, even though you know that it doesn't. At that moment, you play on earth in form in your incarnation, instead of being played upon by all this fleeting world.

A star at dawn, a bubble in a stream, a flash of light in a summer cloud, a flickering lamp, a phantom, a dream. I looked around at my human incarnation, and after all the years of trying to be divine, of clinging to the idea of divinity, suddenly I wanted to be human. I wanted to be into the passions of life and, at the same moment, to have equanimity.

You don't push away the passions of life. You are as Christ said—*in* the world but not *of* the world. You are listening to hear your incarnation and fulfilling it perfectly. There's no being out of form. When you're in form, you're incarnated. Whatcha gonna do? You've got to come to peace with form.

Clinging to Your Beliefs

What happens when you cling to the belief that you are right? You land in righteousness. Most social action is done out of the motive of righteousness, of being on God's side, of doing what seems to be the best for human beings. If you have watched people fight, you often see that they are both feeling very righteous.

In Indian villages in Guatemala, I would meet with people who came out of a culture that was possibly seven thousand years mature, in which they had incredibly deep respect for the god within the human being and they were incredible living-spirit beings. Then I would see Christian missionaries in the same village who had come to teach these heathens how to get to God. I saw the uptightness of the missionaries and their righteousness and the way in which they saw the other people as objects. Living with that kind of confrontation in my heart, and loving Christ at the same moment, I could see how destruction and paranoia are created from a sense of righteousness.

Awakeness is not righteousness; awakeness transcends righteousness. The social action that truly liberates does not come out of righteousness. The minute you cling to your feeling of being righteous, you think of the opponent as unrighteous, and nobody really wants to be thought of as unrighteous. If you deal with another human being and you are considering them unrighteous, you are creating rigidity and tightness in them, which makes it more difficult for them to change.

Power is not the power over people; it is the power that comes from within to do what you do. It's not the power of right and wrong. It's not the power of "We have right on our side." It's merely the power of listening to the flow of things and being within the flow as you see it and letting it pour through you, not deciding necessarily how it comes out.

The question then is whether you identify with your righteousness or whether you identify with your cause or merely act on behalf of your cause. If you act on behalf of your cause, do you identify with being the actor or not? And that comes back to the *Bhagavad Gita*, to not identifying with the actor, which is the essence of karma yoga.

Fear of Change

Do you remember the Chinese curse "May you live in an interesting time"? The question is whether it's a curse or a blessing. See, it's a curse if you're afraid of change. I really see it as a blessing. I look at this body, which is now decaying at a deliciously interesting rate. There are all these big veins and wrinkles and little marks and spots. If I impose upon that all of my social structures, my conceptual things about that's my hand, that means I am wrinkles and blood vessels, and look at how much I value the absence of wrinkles and blood vessels. Am I ready for this? Is there going to be anxiety? Now is this less beautiful?

I have this delicious story that's such fun to tell. It's a little irreverent, but what the hell. . . .

I was invited to give a lecture in Beverly Hills at Saks Fifth Avenue for La Prairie Cosmetics. Now, La Prairie Cosmetics is an old firm which has a sanatorium for health rejuvenation in Switzerland. They have a lot of products coming out and they were marketing a new "antiaging" cream. The previous year I had been a keynote speaker at a conference in New York on aging, so they invited me to speak at the event for fifteen minutes about the wisdom of aging, so it wouldn't just be about money. I probably would've passed it up except they were offering $12,000. It was actually $12,000 for two gigs, but the I. Magnin one didn't happen.

In my righteous image of myself, I thought to myself,

$12,000 is a lot of eyeballs that could be cured through Seva. Can I make a moral statement in which I'm supporting La Prairie so that all those people could see again? It's an interesting ethical dilemma. Then I thought, Look, what does it matter where you teach? You teach where a situation presents itself. My teachings are my teachings. I'm not tailoring the teachings for whom I'm teaching. I'm going to teach my truth. So why not? Aren't the people at Saks Fifth Avenue deprived too?

I agreed to do it and got a suit and a tie and went there. Costume up for the ball. There were tables of maybe ten or twelve people and there was a person from La Prairie at each table to help each person with an individual consultation about how to keep their skin young. I was at the table with the people who were going to be presenters. There were three of us. There was the vice president of La Prairie and then there was a nutritional skin expert. In her demonstration, she stands up and says, "You can all do your own test. Take your skin and pinch it and hold it for five seconds, then let it go and see how fast it goes back." We all put our hands in the middle of the table. I did mine, and after the five seconds my skin didn't go back. In fact, it's still there.

It came my turn to speak, and I stood up and I looked out at my audience. They were serving salad at the luncheon. I saw a number of people with mouths full of lettuce looking up at me with a certain kind of opaque look. It reminded me of when you go out in a field and there's a group of cows and you disturb them at their business and they look up and they're . . . See, that's a little irreverent because they're us too.

The question is, Is change beautiful? Is what changes part of the beauty of nature? Are you part of the beauty of nature and can you allow the changes of aging and delight in them? Can you look for the wisdom inherent in each change rather than resisting it? Can you work to preserve your body and at the same time be ready to let it go? The most remarkable thing is to be at peace with the way of things by cultivating the part of yourself that isn't you anymore, which has nothing to do with time and space, birth and death, coming and going, loss and gain, fame and shame, pleasure and pain. Which ones are you ready for? That would be in the advanced course.

What I said at the luncheon was that aging and death are part of the natural way of things and that if you are buying cosmetics out of fear, then it is not going to give you happiness. If you are buying them out of celebration, that's another thing.

They never invited me back.

Clinging to Thought

A samurai has a commitment that when his master dies, if his master is murdered, his job is to kill the killer of his master. So this samurai's master is murdered and the samurai spends two years looking for the murderer of his master. He finally finds him and chases him up an alley and draws his snickersnee, his sword, to do in the killer, and the killer spits in the samurai's face. The samurai sheaths his sword and turns and walks down the street.

The killer runs after the samurai and says, "I am indeed the killer of your master. I understand the laws. Why didn't you kill me?"

And the samurai says, "Because I got angry."

Can you hear the implications of that story? It's saying, "Do what you do, but if you're doing it out of attachment or clinging mind, watch it." The samurai realizes the nature of the law of karma. He obviously doesn't want the karma on his head of having murdered out of anger. It is the question of any action. Whatever act you perform can be an act of liberation for everyone concerned or an act of entrapment, depending on where your head is at when you perform the act.

If somebody says, "I'm having these terrible thoughts and I don't know why. Would you help me understand why?" I'd say, "I'd rather have you sit down and follow your breath." The breath has no content to it at all. It's just the breath. Better to strengthen the centering, the quieting, the presence, rather than keep strengthening the problem, which keeps being reinforced when you work on the content of the thoughts. And that's a very delicate question. I don't want to undercut times when it's really appropriate to work on problems as content, but for the most part, focusing on the content of thoughts is to me a last strategy. It is a much better strategy to focus on the mechanics of thought rather than the content of thought. That's a very, very critical distinction.

For example, if I'm caught in a lot of thoughts about a relationship, I can go to a therapist, and the therapist will say, "Well, let's talk about your childhood and where the problem came from." That's content. We're dealing with the content of the thoughts. Or I can just see these as more thoughts. Put them in the category of thoughts, not what they're about. They're just thoughts.

My major game in meditation is to extricate awareness from identification with thought or with clinging to thought. In order to do that, I will go into my meditation practice, which in some cases might be following the breath and using one thought to free me from the clinging to other thoughts. I'll start to follow the breath and up will come the thought, What am I going to do about that relationship? See, thought appears. I hear the teacher say, "Return to your breath." I go back to breathing in, breathing out. Then another thought comes and says, God, my life is a mess. Now at that point, you can call a therapist and say, "Let's deal with why my life is a mess." Or you can go back to the breath. Rising . . . falling . . . rising . . . falling . . . rising . . . falling. In other words, you can use the meditative practice to extricate yourself from identification with thoughts, whatever they are, shadowy or not.

There are some thoughts that you won't get rid of that way because they're sort of in a nest or a web of stuff, and then you will approach them in terms of content. But my strategy is to go for the mechanics first and then go to the content later on when some content seems ripe to pick off. Years back I had been in psychoanalysis, and after fifteen years of meditation, certain psychological things were still hung in there. But my awareness had developed great strength, and at that point I went into therapy with a Jungian therapist for about three months. I was ready to pick off a lot of stuff, and that was about as much as I needed of that round.

The more practices you've done, the quicker the working through will be. The predicament of working through with a therapist is that if the therapist is not awakened to these other realms of reality, the therapist thinks that the content is real, while a spiritual perspective sees the content as relatively real. Do you see the difference? So it's really important that you look for therapists or that you work with therapists or that you become a therapist who's rooted in these deeper parts of your being.

Attachment to Perfection

So there was this desire to get on with it, which we interpreted as taking the entire spiritual journey and making it into an achievement course. There is a lovely story about a boy who goes to a Zen master and he says, "Master, I know you have many students. But if I study harder than all the rest of them, how long will it take me to get enlightened?"

The master said, "Ten years."

He said, "Well, if I work day and night and double my efforts, how long will it take?"

The master said, "Twenty years. And with further achievement, thirty years."

He said, "Why do you keep adding years?"

The master said, "Well, since you will have one eye on the goal, there will only be one eye left to have on the work and it will slow you down immeasurably."

And in a way that was the predicament: we got so attached to where we were going that we really had little time to deepen our practice to get there.

Are you attached to perfection? To being perfect? Perfection doesn't happen in form. Form has an imperfection about it. Impeccability means that you're tuned to the harmony, to the Tao, to the way of things, to all of the forces in the universe, out of which comes your action. The action may not be perfect within the context of the situation. I may not be a perfect servant, but I can be impeccable from where I am in terms of the total context in which I exist.

Perfectionism is usually coming out of a compulsive action that comes out of anxiety. It takes a lot of control to make sure everything is okay, to make sure the criteria are clear and that you're doing it absolutely perfectly. Impeccability is a much more liquid thing—continuously tuning in to hear the appropriate action at any moment. It doesn't have to do with perfection as much as doing it appropriately. It may be quite imperfect in the way it's done. I'll do an act that, if I stopped to do it fully, would be perfect.

In the greater warp and weave of things, it's like making a bed. You could spend a lot of time making a bed with perfect hospital corners, but if there are a lot of other things going on in your life, it may not be worth doing it that well. You don't get caught in the perfection of each act. You listen to the appropriateness of it all. That's more what we're talking about when we talk about being impeccable. It's like being in harmony with the forces of the universe.

We begin to appreciate the way in which work on oneself is related to the work for all beings. As one continues to cut through the attachments to self and the attachments to possessions and the attachments that keep one locked into a space, then we get a deeper appreciation of our identity with other human beings. And we begin to find that those actions which we can perform are harmonious with our highest fourth-chakra compassion. And we find that the only things we really want to do are things which are in harmony with that which ends suffering for all beings.

Chapter 4

Mindful Service

Ending suffering for all beings is a mighty tall order. How do you help even one other person without getting lost in being the helper? Or without being overwhelmed and burning out? And what about your own suffering?

In Hinduism, there are different yogic paths for reaching moksha, liberation: bhakti yoga, the path of devotion; gnana yoga, the path of knowledge; raja yoga, the royal path of meditation; and karma yoga, the path of selfless service. Maharajji brought us into a lineage that focused on devotion and selfless service, as exemplified by Hanuman, the monkey god who serves Lord Rama with total devotion. There is a Hanuman murti (consecrated statue) in every one of Maharajji's temples. And the main practice we were given was to chant the "Hanuman Chalisa," forty verses in Hindi in praise of Hanuman.

Those of us who are Maharajji's devotees understand that our dharma is to serve, in whatever capacity suits who we are. Maharajji gave us very few instructions, the basic ones being to love everyone, serve everyone, and remember God. *With their corollary:* tell the truth. *Turns out that's an entire spiritual path, and one that Ram Dass took to heart.*

I'm sitting on a Greyhound bus, reading, when a guy sits down next to me, and he's overweight and taking more of the seat and he's kind of sweaty. I start to pull back a little bit, then he says, "You going to Santa Fe?" I am about to give one of those short answers and then go back to my book when I hear inside my guru saying, "Love everyone, serve everyone, remember God." And the "remember God" does it to me. I think, Well, this is God who's come to me as a teaching. Am I caught in my attachment? What makes me turn off this being? At that point, I put down the book and say, "Yeah, I am going to Santa Fe. Where are you going?"

I realized that my work at any moment is to find in every human being that which is the god in them. That becomes part of my work. Then I have to deal with "serve everyone." Somebody asks me to do something and they're asking me out of a very worldly desire on their part. Well, am I supposed to fulfill that? Is that what "serve" means? Does it mean to do anything anybody wants me to do? Or is it to serve the god in each human being? Sometimes I can say no to somebody and I understand that I'm serving them. I have to wrestle with that all the time. What is service? What's the purest service? Whom are you serving?

You can't serve man and God at the same moment, so you're listening to how you can serve the god in every human being, not necessarily the worldly illusion that each person is caught in. But that's a very subtle thing, and that's why these three instructions are so beautiful, because they keep you working all the time to understand what they mean.

Being Good

In most of the work I do to help other people, I'm coming in doing good works and everybody says, "Ram Dass is so good." And I am. I'm really good. It's a great role in the world, like liquid grace all the time. But there's a place in me that still rips it off, that still is somebody doing something, and therefore whomever I'm doing it to becomes somebody to whom I've done something. In other words, it distances me from my beloved.

In the sixties, I became a renunciate for a while. A horny one, but a renunciate. A renunciate who, in effect, said the world of stuff is so seductive that I have got to get away from it for a while. I've got to stop reading *The New York Times*. I've got to pull back for a moment in order to hear the voice within. So I pulled back. When you pull back, you begin to think that this plane of reality is somehow less. You get caught in that. After a while I saw that if I went to act from where I was, the likelihood was I was going to create suffering even if I was attempting to do good.

For example, giving somebody food. Well, of course you want to give people food, but where you give the people food from determines whether you feed their stomach or feed their freedom. I saw that I was feeding stomachs but not freedom, and that it wasn't an either/or. It was a both/and, but I hadn't gotten my act together because I was still somebody doing something. So I got into a strategy—we can't do good until we are good, and then we be good, and then good happens. Got that? We can't do good till we be good, and when we be good, then good happens. You don't do it, but it happens anyway. It's the Tao. One does nothing and nothing is left undone.

What I'm basically talking about is learning to live simultaneously on two planes of awareness, so that your actions are not coming in reaction to the forms around you but out of emptiness. It is coming also out of another plane behind that, where there isn't form. It's so hard because of the seductiveness of the suffering and the wanting to do something about it. You get caught in *doing* and don't cultivate *being* because you're a good person.

In the late sixties, there were the people who said, "Look, you can't wait to do good. Go *do* good; the hell with *being* good." The others said, "We better get on with our being or else we're not going to do much good." We all did our part, and that was all the movements and all the stuff that went down. By the mid-seventies, we realized that we were all trapped in our practices. The doers were burning out; the be-ers were feeling cut off from the life force of the universe because they were pushing away the world.

I realized that if Buddha is right—that attraction or aversion of mind is the cause of suffering—and if I am averse to my own passions or my own pain or the world's pain or anything, it's got me. It's got me. You can't be phony holy. You can't push it away. You can't go to la-la land. So at that point, I flipped around and said, "Okay, my yoga of getting free now will be through being in the world." That's what I was told to do and I might as well do it. When I had asked my guru, "How do I get enlightened?" his answer was "Feed people."

I figured it got lost in the translation, so I tried again: "How do I know God?" He said, "Serve people."

Turned out that he was right. That was my way. For me, it is a strategy, a practice, a path that involves service as a vehicle to transcend dualism. I'm named Ram Dass, servant of God, which is a name of Hanuman. You've got to understand that in Maharajji's lineage, Hanuman [an incarnation of Lord Shiva] is a great being who takes the form of a monkey in order to serve Ram, who is God.

All the bhakti, or devotional, rays that come out from God have different relationships. Some of them are related to God as lover to beloved, some of them are related to God as your father, God as your mother, God as your child. Hanuman serves God as servant to master. But the words "service" and "master" are strange in the West. It's a servant problem. Hanuman is known as the breath of Ram. Hanuman is as close to God as God's breath. At one point in the Hindu epic of *The Ramayana*, Ram says to Hanuman, "Who are you?" And Hanuman says, "When I don't know who I am, I serve you. When I know who I am, I am you."

Compassionate Action

I see three levels of compassionate action: One, you do compassionate action as best you can as an exercise to come closer to God, to spirit, to awareness, to the One. The next level is you start to appreciate that you're part of something larger than yourself. You are an instrument of God and you begin to feel that identity. No longer are you doing it to get there; you're now doing it as an instrument. The third one is where you lose self-consciousness and then you are God manifesting, part of the hand of God, and then you're not doing anything and it's God manifesting. I can feel those levels.

Rather than coming in with a program that defines reality so rigidly, I saw that the deepest part of the teaching is in the statement "Out of emptiness arises compassion." When I am empty of my separateness for a moment, I experience the totality. I am the totality. And out of that intuitive gestalt comes a response that doesn't ignore that suffering or that joy or that reality or that possibility. What a great teaching.

In India, I was walking down a line of leper beggars and I had some different denomination coins in my hand. Some were rupee coins and some were paise, worth about a tenth of a cent. I had all these coins, and here was a line of about a hundred lepers with their bowls. I started down the row and I was so freaked by the situation that my mind started to wonder whom to give which coins to. If you're missing a nose, is that worth fifty paise or is it worse if you don't have any arms, which might be worth a rupee? A rupee and a half if your face has been eaten away? I couldn't look at anybody. I was so freaked. That scene was so impossible I flipped out of my mind.

When your rational mind gets blown, you are forced back into your intuitive heart. I walked down the line of lepers, letting my intuition decide which coin to give to which leper. I looked into all their eyes and I didn't see rejection or judgment or anything that would create guilt in me. I had this beautiful contact with each being. When I got to the end of the line, I had no more coins. It had been a rewarding experience rather than one that completely would've burned me out had I stayed in my mind of deciding "How much?" and "Should I?"

and "Can I?" and "Can't I?" It turns out the lepers have a union and they share all their coins, but I didn't know that, so I got the teaching.

Serving *Us*

You have to anticipate that until the moment when you are fully enlightened, your serving is going to have a complex set of motives connected with it. Partly it's going to be done in order to alleviate your own guilt that you are not suffering the way that person is suffering. Partly it's a sense of righteousness about the unfairness of the world. Partly it's in order to be loved by somebody: you serve them, you help them. There's a whole range of human motives that are engaged in a relationship with another person that have to do with your own separateness. As long as you are identified with your separateness, those motives are going to be called into play. If you get busy judging yourself for them and reacting against them, all you do is lock them in and complicate the dynamics of the situation. That's all part of the psychosocial part of serving.

As you work on your consciousness and extricate your awareness from so much heavy identification with your own separateness, you realize after a while that whom you're serving is not *her* or *him* or *them*. You begin to feel the nature of *interbeing*, as Thich Nhat Hanh talks about, the interconnections among things, the unitive nature of the universe, the feeling that I am part of everything, I am one with everything. And you realize that what you're serving is the suffering in *us*. So a different motivation for serving is serving *us*.

As that quality deepens, then when somebody else is suffering, it's not somebody else. It's that part of *us* that is suffering. It's very much like this hand is in the fire and this other hand reaches over and pulls it out. This hand doesn't have to turn to that hand and say thank you, because they are both hands of the same organism. In that sense, from a transcendent point of view, helping is an internal matter. You're not doing it for somebody else.

When you're in a relation of helping, the very act of helping isolates me from you; it's making me the helper and you the helped. However, when you are helping from a transcendent point of view, there is just the helping act. Here we are. Who's getting helped remains quite unclear because, if it's working, since I am you as well as me and you are me as well as you, I am experiencing being helped as much as I am experiencing helping. Can you hear that?

You meet another person and, look, there's food and there's a hungry belly and there's food and there's a hand. Let's put the hand into the food and put the food into the belly and whose belly it is and whose hand it is don't matter. It is a process that you and I are in together, and under those conditions, when your mind is in that space, the very act of helping brings people together.

The Impersonal Nature of Society

When you have surrendered completely into God, you find yourself in the service of all that exists. It becomes your joy and recreation. At that point you begin to examine your own actions of life in relation to the nature of the suffering of others, and that's when something like voluntary simplicity starts to come into your life. It isn't worth having that extra thing, because when I have that extra thing, it makes me turn off other people in order to hold on to that thing. So you start to reorganize the way you use your economics and the way you live your life.

A lot of us are just beginning to learn how to do that. We grew up with a middle-class vision. We grew up with this, we have a right to this, our parents had this, we can have this. But when you grow up in an extended village and everybody knows everybody and is related, it's very hard to be sitting at the table eating when somebody you've known all your life walks up to the table and they haven't eaten in eight or nine days and they're emaciated and hungry. Would you say, "Excuse me, would you go away? I'm busy eating."

In a way, it's the impersonality of society that allows us to treat other people as if they're not our family. We're very slow to get out of our egocentric predicament, to have empathy for the situation in a broader way. When I came back from India, a group of people came to my father's farm in the summer of '69 and pretty soon a hundred people were camping on the estate. My father was very generous. He let everybody stay there in tents on his golf course and he was very, very loving. When it rained, people would sleep in this huge barn that held a pool table and a Ping-Pong table and a pipe organ and all this stuff.

One morning, my father, who was feeling very beneficent about having taken care of all these people, walked into the barn and all these bodies were everywhere. He saw that somebody had a dog and the dog had defecated on the floor. He turned to a fellow and said, "Say, would you get some paper and clean that up?" And the fellow said, "It wasn't my dog." My father came out completely bewildered. He had been busy saying he has all these people who love each other and it's all one. He was opening to that. Then he faced what was there—a tremendous amount of "It's not my dog," "It's not my glass," and so on.

We're just learning how to play. It's like what we're learning about ecology. You can't go and soil your nest. I remember giving a lecture in Berkeley, California, for several thousand people, and everybody was full of love and light and it was all beautiful. When they all left and got into their old Volkswagen buses and started to drive away, all those microbuses had stickers on them that said "love everyone" and "peace" and "truth" and "beauty" and "God is good" and "sex is free" and all sorts of things. I was behind one of these Volkswagen buses at a red light and I was feeling very good about aren't we wonderful and love everyone. Suddenly I saw somebody throw a paper cup out of the driver's-side window. I felt so crushed. I mean, it was like somebody had walked into my living room and spit on the floor.

Whose ground is that, theirs or ours?

I guess what many of us are finally beginning to realize, maybe a little too late or maybe too slowly, is that *the earth is our earth. It's our home and the people on it are our family.* We are shifting very slowly in our consciousness from a nation-state mentality, from the mentality of they are *them* in developing countries to it's all *us*. Slowly we have to reinvest a world consciousness, a world government, a world political structure.

Becoming an Instrument of Change

Gandhi said that when you surrender completely into God, you find yourself in the service of all that exists. He surrendered into the pain of India and he became India's pain and India's healing instead of somebody separate. Each of us has a unique predicament in our lives and we have to listen to hear which way will serve as our vehicle for embracing the suffering of the world around us.

If you have to turn your head away from suffering in order to be happy, you are standing on tiptoe, off-balance. You're not free, and that isn't true joy. The joy is in embracing, with your heart open, the world just as it is, with all of it, all of it, all of it, with the hurt and the beauty and the joy and the life and the death and all of it. In fact, every emotion is present all the time in the fullness of the moment. You no longer are in the dualism of dark versus light, good versus bad, happy versus sad. You're not pushing away one end of a polarity in order to grab the other. You're embracing all of the stuff into the oneness.

Here's an example to give you a feeling of the way in which this process works. Mike Jeffrey was a lawyer from Los Angeles. He was in a very bad automobile accident while in Boston and I went to see him in the hospital. He was a little disillusioned about law, and he had a nice heart and he had read something of mine. We talked in his hospital room and he decided to go to India.

Mike went to India in the early seventies and ended up at the temple of Neem Karoli Baba, my guru. He was a very sweet, pure man, and Maharajji gave him the name Ravi Das. Pretty soon he was in the back of the ashram washing pots and planting flowers and helping out around the place. He started to learn herbal medicine and helped the local people with various herbs. He learned Hindi. Usually in Hindu temples Brahmins do the cooking. They don't let Westerners cook because we're not pure enough. But he was very pure and they at least let him do the pots and some of the cooking. When I was at the temple, all of us would be trying to be at my guru's feet all the time while Ravi Das would be out back washing pots. I thought, What a sweet, simple man he is. He's a true servant. Isn't that lovely?

Then my guru left his body. Ravi Das didn't leave India; he stayed on at the temple washing pots and cleaning up and doing all the menial work. I thought, He's a lawyer and he's very intelligent. I wonder if he's lost it somehow. Do you think he's going to end up just being a pot washer? I mean, it's nice, but really . . .

Finally he got thrown out of India when they wouldn't extend his visa any longer. He came back to Los Angeles and hung out at his parents' home for a while, not quite knowing what to do. The temple in India had been his life. Then he saw a little ad in the paper that said a public defender was needed for the Alaskan Natives in Barrow, Alaska. He thought, Why not? Maybe that's my way to serve.

He went up to Barrow, and within a few years he had become a member of the Alaska Native dance troop. He went on fishing expeditions. He defended the Alaska Natives' whaling grounds against the oil interests. And he became a deeply loved member of the Native community. Then he was chosen by the governor of Alaska as the youngest superior court judge in Alaska, where he makes decisions about people's lives and is recognized for his purity and his caring. From pot washer to judge, he found his way in each situation to serve and listen and feel, leading a life of service, of love, of devotion, of working on himself, of quieting.

Our lives don't have to have a showbiz kind of service. They can be the simple qualities of service that arise in the family or in the person down the street. We must find a way to integrate spirituality into our daily lives. Bring into it the equanimity and the joy and the awe and the ability to look suffering in the eye and embrace it into yourself without averting your glance. I work with AIDS patients and I'm holding somebody and my heart is breaking because I love this person and they are suffering so much, with fissures in their rectum and with social ostracism and all of that shit. I'm crying with him. And at the same moment inside of me is this equanimity and joy. The paradox is almost too much for me to be able to handle.

But that is what real helping is about. If all you do is get caught in the suffering, all you're doing is digging everybody's hole deeper. Finally, you work on yourself spiritually as an offering to your fellow beings. Because until you have cultivated that quality of peace and equanimity and love and joy and presence and honesty and truth and simplicity, all of your acts are colored by your attachments. You can't wait to be enlightened to act. So you use your acts as ways of working on yourself.

Burnout

Burnout is a major issue in serving. When you go to help somebody, one of the biggest traps is called the "helper's prison." Being a *helper* is to get caught in thinking you're helping somebody. If you think you're helping somebody, you are cutting yourself off from the person you're helping by identifying with the role of being a helper. Actually, when I am helping somebody, helping is happening and the helping brings us together rather than separates us.

The thing that catches you in your role of being a helper

is wondering whether you're adequate, whether your tools are good enough, and also your fear of getting too involved with the helpless for fear you'll get trapped and your heart will hurt too bad. That's a big one. It's a certain set of psychological things you have in your mind to keep yourself distant from the people you're helping. Like pity. When you pity somebody, your mind is pushing them away. It's different from just being with them, allowing it, acknowledging it. Yes, your heart hurts and their heart hurts, and we're still right here.

It's interesting to see how helping can bring people closer together. One of the hardest of the acts in helping is to realize your limitations and be able to say no without closing your heart. The question is where the depth of the no comes out of. If it comes out of your mind, it's going to end up cutting you off from everybody. If the no is rooted in the nature of your being, it's because you're resting in your being and the no is just the way of things. You don't identify with the no.

Compassion fatigue? Well, fatigue is a clue to us that we're doing it from a level that isn't yet conscious enough. It's showing that we are still identified with thinking we are the actor and we're still very much attached to the effects of our acts. *The Bhagavad Gita*'s instruction is not to be either of those. You can use the fatigue to show you where you are still stuck. I still get fatigued from too much action. You are feeding on your actions so that your actions are feeding you, giving you more and more energy. Maharajji slept two hours a night, if that. He was full of energy all the time because there was no attachment. He was fully there, an interflow of energy back and forth between him and the universe. My thing is to spiral, so I pull back and then I go do a meditation retreat or I go and play for a while or I do something to give myself some space. As part of my effectiveness as a human being, I need to do that.

Look at the way in which your service or caring action is somehow based on your own guilt that you are not enough, all the ways in which you help somebody and you do something to bring about an effect. If the effect doesn't happen, you end up interpreting it as your fault. The concept in India of doing one's dharma is you do what is appropriate for you to do in view of your skills, your opportunities, your talents. You do it consciously and as an offering into the relief of suffering, but it's God's will as to what happens next. A successful outcome is not in your hands; it's in God's hands.

I am what I am, and because of what I am, I do this and this is what happens. This is the teaching of dharma. My job is to do nothing so that all this can happen without me getting in the way of it by thinking I'm doing something. If it's working all right, you will hear the message as clearly as it can come through me. What you do with it is your karmic predicament, not mine. If I'm attached to what you do with it, I will burn out. Can you hear that?

Think of the trap of being a doctor in this society—"Doctor, cure me"—or a therapist or psychotherapist, where somebody comes and says, "I am paying you money to cure me." You understand that all you are going to do is offer your being to this person and create an environment in which they can cure themselves. But if you say to them at the outset, "I can't cure you; you can cure yourself," they probably won't pay you. It's interesting what kind of contracts you can enter into and how much the contract traps you into identifying with being somebody that's supposed to do something for somebody else, how quickly that burns you out.

What you *do* is never enough. What you *are* is always enough. Very often when you're with somebody, you have nothing to offer them, then you have to let go and let go and let go and offer your being, which turns out to be what it's about and turns out to be enough.

Perfect Service

Maharajji kept saying to me, "Ram Dass, don't you see, it's all perfect." Yet Maharajji spent all of his life in that embodiment, being there for people, constantly feeding people, taking care of people, advising people, making do for people. I saw in him the coming together of social action and emptiness, the space from which you see the perfection. It's the clear discriminating awareness from which perfection spreads out before you as all the universe of forms, from the original particles as they merged together to your own mind, to the violence and the death and the pain, all of it.

The only perfect service is called "selfless service"—service without self-consciousness, service without a mediating thought form of "I ought to serve" or "Look, I am serving." As long as you are self-consciously watching yourself serve, the service is always going to be less than perfect. "What do you do?" I serve.

Let me tell you, any definition of who you are is a drag. I would let it go as fast as you possibly could because one of the very exciting things is to find out you don't have to be anybody. It's nobody who gets in the door of heaven. And that's why spiritual work equals social action from my point of view. The social-action spiritual-journey path to me is all of one thing. It comes down to what is sometimes called "karma yoga."

The game is to bear the unbearable with a giggle, trusting your inner wisdom. The cause of suffering is the clinging of mind. That's why ultimately you work on yourself, so that every human relationship you're in, whether it's child or wife or competitor or enemy, is not a violent one but is rooted in the oneness that embraces both beings. The art is to delight in the dance, and out of you will come actions not out of *ought* or *should*, but out of the essence of *what is*.

The statement in the Tao is "One does nothing and nothing is left undone," meaning you're getting very tired of being somebody doing something. There's a whole other way of being in which you are the thing itself and whatever happens, happens. It's the compassion that arises out of emptiness. It's the discriminating wisdom that you see when you stop trying so hard to be good, to be right, to be just, to be compassionate.

Joan Baez found her commitment to nonviolence pushed to the limits in the ruins of Sarajevo. Everywhere she went, her strong silver voice was accompanied by the staccato sounds of shelling from the hills around the bloodied city. She went, she said, not with any answers but as a nonviolent response to what was happening there. She wanted to share her life and her music and be a witness to people who were undergoing such tremendous suffering. She told me, "The best thing I could have done was just to be there because they are, for the most part, no longer afraid of dying. They are afraid of being forgotten."

As Baez trudged through the muddy landing strip on her way out of Sarajevo, a young woman who attended the concert came up to her and said, "Thank you for coming. You have brought us life." That's all Joan needed to know. It had been the right thing to do.

How do you bring life to somebody? How does that infusion take place between people? The ability for two people to fulfill their roles inherent in their relationship without being trapped by them so they meet behind their roles, they meet in being together. That is an infusion. What a play, what a dance! As the poet Rabindranath Tagore said, "I slept and dreamt that life was joy. I awoke and saw that life was service. I acted and behold, service was joy."

You are ready to be an instrument of the relief of suffering.

I feel so connected to Maharajji. I feel that he's drawing me into it at the rate I'm being drawn in. I can feel that of my brothers and sisters in Seva, as they open their hearts and their beings. We all keep forming these relationships that allow us to hear how to serve more and more clearly. We keep merging into this deeper commitment to our fellow human beings that comes out of a more natural part of our compassionate heart. Rilke has that line in his poem "Elegy X" about seeing "behind the billboard" at the edge of town. It's like you see behind the illusion and you see beyond it and you get this incredible feeling that you've been privy to seeing into the mind and the breath of God.

REFLECTION ON SUFFERING

by Jack Kornfield

Ram Dass always enjoyed very close ties with our Buddhist "cousins," especially the three Westerners who were largely responsible for bringing the Buddhist practices of Vipassana meditation (insight, including mindfulness) and metta (lovingkindness) to the West after receiving their training in the East—Sharon Salzberg and Joseph Goldstein, who cofounded the Insight Meditation Society (IMS) in Barre, Massachusetts, and Jack Kornfield, a founding teacher of IMS and Spirit Rock Meditation Center in Woodacre, California.

Jack trained as a Buddhist monk in the monasteries of Thailand, India, and Burma. He has taught meditation internationally since 1974, holds a PhD in clinical psychology, and is the author of over a dozen books on the Buddhist path, such as No Time Like the Present *and* After the Ecstasy, the Laundry.

Jack and his wife, Trudy Goodman, a Vipassana teacher and the founding teacher of InsightLA, frequently taught with Ram Dass at his annual retreats in Maui and have continued to do so since Ram Dass left his body in 2019.

Here, Jack elaborates on the Buddhist view of dukkha, *suffering, as the stimulus for awakening to compassion.*

When I was first in Buddhist monasteries in Thailand and Burma, I was taught three keys to the basic nature of life: everything is *anicca*, all is impermanent; everything is *dukkha*, which means "unsatisfactory"; and everything is *anatta*, which means "selfless," empty like a dream. They are gateways to liberation. If you can see these qualities, you see with the eyes of wisdom.

Dukkha means all things are insecure and uncertain; sometimes this is translated as "suffering." All we have to do is turn on the news to see our human struggles with continuing wars, climate change, pandemics, and the scourge of racism to see dukkha. Aging, sickness, and death are dukkha. Grasping, clinging, and fear are dukkha. These are an inevitable part of human incarnation, folks.

So when the Buddha attained enlightenment under the bodhi tree, he saw beings everywhere wanting to be happy, yet often doing the very things that made them unhappy. The great heart of compassion arose in him and tears rolled down his cheeks. Seeing the suffering of the world, he began to shine his compassion in every direction. Let me help beings be free so that they can live with peaceful and loving hearts amidst it all.

He explained that there are three kinds of dukkha. There's anicca, which is the dukkha of change—the unstoppable cycles of joy and sorrow, praise and blame, gain and loss, pleasure and pain, fame and disrepute. We try to hold on to the pleasure and joy, but it doesn't last. Of course, the good thing is that when things are terrible, they don't last either. You can't hold on.

The second kind of dukkha is the dukkha of physical and mental pain. We live in a culture that basically wants to sell you a prescription, a painkiller, the moment you're a little uncomfortable. Good luck. It doesn't work that way. My friend the surgeon general of the United States said that more than half of what comes into the hospitals and clinics across America is really based on emotional pain and suffering. So this is the second kind of dukkha, physical and mental pain. You all know it because it's part of incarnation. We all have it.

The third kind is called "samsara dukkha." *Samsara* means the cycles of existence, the whole world of duality. Samsara dukkha is the nature of things. We have a globe and a world and a moon and a solar system and galaxies, all a play of duality; there's light and dark, birth and death. There is unbearable beauty, amazing beauty, and an ocean of tears. Built into this human life are birth and death. Did you never see a man or a woman aged, bent down and walking with a cane, or sick and lying in bed? Did you never see a corpse after their life energy has passed from the body? Did the thought never happen to come to you, Oh, this will happen to me too?

When you really see anicca and dukkha deeply, this makes room for something new to be born. You begin to trust the process. The waves of life and the emotions come and there's sadness and fear and gain and loss, and if you allow them all, letting them open in a spacious way, if you stay with it, it all passes and there you are, still the loving witness of it all. So anicca is the doorway to trust, and dukkha gives birth to compassion. Your grief becomes a doorway. They come together to make a courageous heart.

There's a story of an old Hasidic rabbi who used to talk about the practice of prayer and meditation. He would say, "When you meditate, when you pray, when you offer your prayers, when you recite them, feel them and place them on your heart." One day a student said, "Rabbi, why do you always use that strange phrase, 'place them *on* your heart'? Shouldn't we put them *in* our heart?" The rabbi got quiet and said, "It's not us who can put them in the heart. Our practice is to recite them and place them on the heart so that someday, when the heart breaks, they will fall in." This is how grief and dukkha become the doorway to compassion.

You see a hungry child, a painful injustice, an act of violence to an innocent person and your heart goes out. You want to help. The profound reality of suffering is an invitation to step out of the fiction of separateness, grasping at what is called the "small sense of self" or the "body of fear," where we are frightened or selfish or self-centered or cut off. This is not who we are. We know there is a reality beyond this. We feel it walking in the high mountains or making love or being there at the mystery of the birth of a child or the death of a human being. All of a sudden we step out of time-bound consciousness, the separateness, and feel ourselves part of the turning of the seasons of life. You can feel it on retreat. You're doing walking meditation and all of a sudden you realize you're not doing it. It's all just doing it itself. It's amazing. One of my teachers explained this as "No self, no problem." More self, more clinging; more self-centered, more problem.

Accepting dukkha, anicca, and anatta, you can live in a timeless present.

I loved watching Ram Dass in the last years of his life. He was there in that wheelchair in a broken body where he couldn't move one arm and one leg, where he had aphasia and he couldn't really speak fluently. He grappled to find words. He had multiple infections and physical traumas and bedsores at times. Yet he was about the happiest person I'd ever been with. Really joyful amidst all the paralysis and aphasia. How can you be so joyful? He said, "I am loving awareness. I love it all—the joy, the sorrow, the birth, the death, the spring, and the winter."

So when you understand that this is our incarnation, there comes a beautiful sense of freedom. The heart changes when we come to terms with dukkha and say, "Yes, that's part of incarnation." Loss and change and pain and suffering and gain and pleasure all are woven together. It becomes an invitation to freedom. It is here always, a joy that comes when we see with the eyes of wisdom and the great heart of compassion and trust. We can let go and become the loving awareness that holds it all.

Oh, nobly born, remember this teaching for now and forever. Your joy, your peace, your acceptance, your flexibility, your non-rigidity, your openness, even with your own foibles, like I with mine, all of those things finally held in the great heart of compassion.

Teach yourself peace. Pass it on.

COMPASSION PRACTICES

by Mirabai Bush

Mirabai Bush is a devotee of Neem Karoli Baba and spent time with him in India from 1971 to 1972. Along with Ram Dass, she is the coauthor of Compassion in Action *and* Walking Each Other Home. *In 2024, she retired as chair of the Love Serve Remember Foundation, dedicated to preserving and continuing the teachings of Neem Karoli Baba and Ram Dass.*

Mirabai is senior fellow and founder of the Center for Contemplative Mind in Society, which encourages contemplative practice and perspective in American life in order to create a more just, compassionate, and reflective society. Mirabai has also worked with Google on a workplace course called Search Inside Yourself and with the US Army on a program for chaplains and medics. She is the former director of the Seva Foundation's Guatemala Brillando project, which supports sustainable agriculture and integrated community development.

She is the editor of Contemplation Nation, *coauthor of* Contemplative Practices in Higher Education, *and author of* Working with Mindfulness *(CD).*

Mirabai often led the following compassion practices at Open Your Heart in Paradise retreats in Maui with Ram Dass, an excellent antidote to "us" versus "them."

Compassion can be cultivated, so that when you experience suffering in another, you are more likely to have a compassionate response. So we're going to do two short practices.

The Practice of Self-Compassion

You can do this practice at any time by putting both hands on your heart and pausing for a moment. Feel the warmth that's coming from your hands toward yourself. Allow yourself to feel a warm care from yourself. Breathe deeply in and out, and speak to yourself silently or out loud in a warm and caring tone.

First bring to mind something that is difficult for you now, something that's hard for you. Maybe you're worried about something, maybe you've been hurt by somebody. Maybe you're feeling insecure. You say to yourself, "This is a moment of suffering for me" or "I'm having a hard time right now." Everybody has these hard times. Then simply say, "May I give myself the love and compassion that I need right now, like I would do for a friend."

Continue to breathe in and out, and feel the warmth of your hands and allow yourself to feel cared for, to feel loved. For a few moments, remember Ram Dass's basic message: I am loving awareness. Keep silently repeating "I am loving awareness. I am loving awareness." Then slowly open your eyes. Come back into the room, and take a moment to tell yourself that you can do this at any time, especially when you're aware that you're feeling hurt or it's hard for you. The truth is we always have something going on, so you can do it at any time.

Just Like Me Practice

The next practice, Just Like Me, is learning to be compassionate to yourself. You don't want to be suffering; you would love to have your suffering relieved. That understanding is what leads you to want to be compassionate for others. The other part of it is recognizing the way in which others are just like us. Everyone wants to be happy. Nobody wants to suffer. We spend a lot of time these days looking at all of our differences. That's really important and we need to keep honoring that diversity. We honor our unique, diverse selves by remembering how much we are alike at the same time that we are really different.

It's a short practice, but a deep one.

If you are feeling that you don't want to do it with a partner, you don't have to because it's just as good to practice doing it by yourself at home alone, but doing it with a partner will teach you something different, and it doesn't really matter if it's someone you don't know at all. In a way, it's more interesting to do it with someone you don't know.

You'll be looking in the eyes of the other person. It's sometimes difficult to look straight in somebody's eyes for the eight minutes or so of this practice because if you're just staring at their eyes, you start blinking. So the best way to do it is to look in the center of the person's forehead. That way you can hold their whole being and your gaze doesn't get strange and you don't start feeling like looking away.

Things arise during practice that we can never predict. If it's too much to look at another person for that time, you're free to close your eyes or to look down, drop your gaze. What I'm saying is this is totally safe, but I want it to also *feel* safe. You're not being forced to do anything here. This is just to help us appreciate each other.

We're going to begin with eyes closed and quieting down, letting go. Being here, letting it all go. Breathing in and breathing out.

Now open your eyes and notice that across from you is another human being, just like you. Have someone read the following phrases out loud so you and your partner can repeat them to yourself, silently:

This person has a body and a mind, just like me.
This person has thoughts and feelings, just like me.
This person has been sad in their life, just like me.
This person has worried about things, just like me.
This person has been angry, just like me.
This person has had physical pain and suffering at some time, just like me.
This person has had mental pain and suffering, just like me.
This person has felt unsafe at times, just like me.
This person has struggled to do their work well, just like me.
This person has been disappointed by life at times, just like me.
This person will die, just like me.
And this person wants to be free from pain and suffering, just like me.
This person wants to be happy and peaceful, just like me.
This person wants to make a good contribution to the world, just like me.

This person wants to be healthy and strong, just like me.
This person wants to be safe everywhere, just like me.
This person wants to be free in every way, just like me.

Now, wishing well to this person.

May you be happy.
May you be free from pain and suffering.
May your life have ease in it.
May you not always have to struggle so much.
May there be joy in your life.
May you be loved.
May you be free in every way.

And now, in any way that feels appropriate, thank your partner for doing this with you.

PART II

Self-Awareness

A human being is a part of the whole, called by us "Universe," a part limited in time and space. He experiences himself, his thoughts and feelings as something separate from the rest—a kind of optical delusion of his consciousness. The striving to free oneself from this delusion is the one issue of true religion.

—*Albert Einstein*

Chapter 5

Time to Go Home

In part 1 of this book, Ram Dass looked at the way in which we cling to our beliefs and how judgment separates "us" from "them." Here, in part 2, Ram Dass explores how separation fragments our inner lives as well.

Most spiritual paths talk about the journey to enlightenment, when we will fully realize that we are one with it all. To be aware that we are all individuals and, at the same time, one with the greater community of sentient beings. To feel in our hearts that at last we are home. As Ram Dass says in Polishing the Mirror*: "If I am not at home anywhere in the universe, I've got a problem. If I say I can only be home here, but not there, what is home? Home is where the heart is."*

Home is the place where there is no separation from others and no separation from self. How did we get so far from home that we find ourselves internally torn between head and heart, between role and soul? In this chapter, Ram Dass takes us through an overview of what we look like when we are far from wholeness, and he shows us how, as our incarnations advance, we finally arrive home.

There was a moment when I was on tour once for a very long time, it seemed like twenty-five years, and I came to another Ramada Inn in some city somewhere. I came into the room, and it had the usual accoutrements of a Ramada Inn. I sat down on the plastic couch and I took my holy pictures and put them on the plastic table, and I sat there. I wanted to quiet myself before I went in and unwrapped the bar of soap. I thought to myself, Well, a couple more weeks and I can go home.

I heard myself think that and I thought, Wow! Am I creating suffering for myself? So I got up and went outside, closed the door, and walked down the hall. I turned around and came back, opened the door, and yelled, "I'm home!" Enough of waiting to go home. Why don't I start out as if I'm home?

So what is the journey that will take you, whoever you may be right now, home?

In the Beginning

For this moment, let us think of *you* as an entity, an entity that exists over a large expanse of time and that goes through experience after experience. Time after time you've been born into an identity and each time you thought that when you died you wouldn't exist anymore. Then you died, and here you still were. Now here you are in the middle of one of these rounds. The quality of this round is that it seems very real. You really think you're here. You really think this body is who you are, this personality is who you are. And when this body dies, you figure that's it. With your intellect, many of you know that isn't it, but with your gut, it's still it.

In the beginning, you were a being totally in harmony with everything around you, no differentiation, no separation, perfect flow. We will, to give it a familiarity, call it the Garden of Eden. There was nothing separate. Everything flowed together. All the parts were not identified with their separateness, but with the One. Then something happened that had to do with the apple—the development of duality, of subject/object. It led to the fig leaf. It led to God saying, "Who told you you were naked?" It's the moment of separation. It's the moment in which the separate entity knows it *knows*, rather than just *being*. Do you understand what I'm talking about?

Separation

Separateness. You ate of the apple of knowledge. That's the beginning of lust. The beginning of greed. The beginning of doubt. The beginning of all of the effects of separation from the One. Each life you enter through the womb, build an ego structure that tells you that you are a separate entity, and spend your life trying to gain, through your own personal power, the reexperiencing of that perfect harmony that you once knew before you became separate.

Achievement, orgasm, adventure—all of it designed for that moment of merging, that moment of transcendence. Trying to create through your mastery and control your own heaven on earth, with you as God. Trying to optimize the strategy of your life so you gain as many of those moments that feel like how it used to be, that feel like you're as back at the Source as possible, back home.

Soon enough, you have become a master of the game of using your power to gain gratification. You function under the philosophy that *more is better*. More is better two ways: One, thickening every experience. So if a bath is good, a bath with incense is better. A bath with incense and bath oil; a bath with incense, bath oil, and someone else in the bath; incense, bath oil, a partner, stereo earphones, wine and cheese, preceded by an oil rub. On and on, more is better, thicker, richer, more and more. Trying to get all your senses gratified simultaneously. The *feelings* of life. So you drive through the night with your quadraphonic sound in your car, smoking, talking, being sexually aroused, speeding, and you say, "This is life." It's true, isn't it?

Then the other way that more is better is getting the rushes closer together. Like you're in the middle of dinner and you're wondering about what you'll have for dessert. During dessert, you're already anticipating coffee, but what will you do afterward? We'll go bowling, and then maybe a movie. How about an ice-cream soda, a ride, music? Let's make love. What's in the refrigerator? And on and on it goes. Rush after rush. Between every rush, in which you are lost in the rush and you have lost your self-consciousness into the experience, between every one of those rushes is that little panic of separation, and thus the seeking of the next rush.

If you're really good, you can get them closer and closer together. You can almost have the illusion there is no space. You figure, If I had more money and more power, I could do it. . . . But it's not going to work. You've done it hundreds of times, life after life after life. If only I were this, then I would . . . If only I make this much money and have two cars and a winter vacation and a fur coat and insurance policies and my children are secure, then I will experience that. We go through it again and again and again.

Eventually you recognize that Christ was, in fact, correct when he said, "Lay not up your treasures upon earth, where moth and rust doth corrupt." Despair. Everything you could figure out to do didn't do it. You drank it, crocheted it, ate it, smoked it, shot it, read it, looked at it, caressed it, and it didn't do it. For a moment, it did. But here you are, "Stuck Inside of Mobile with the Memphis Blues Again."

It's Time to Wake Up

You got lost in the illusion. *Waah*, I want more. Give me more. You're a good child. You're taught how to be a good human being. You live life. But somewhere in the middle of this particular round, there is a parting of the veil, a seeing through the illusion of separateness. There is a moment of awakening. There is a point at which you begin to know or sense who you are.

It's the moment when you see that who you thought you were is not really who you are. That moment of awakening may have come through a traumatic experience, through a crisis, through a death in the family, through falling through space, through a motorcycle accident. It could come at a moment of sexual orgasm. It could come as you're approaching death. It could come at the birth of your child. It could come when the despair and depression get deep because you see the emptiness of the entire game you've been playing. There are many, many,

many conditions when you are ready for that to happen. It's called the "initial satori experience" in Zen. It's the moment in which there is a moment of clarity and you see through the dance, but most people are busy denying those moments because they don't fit in with the model you have of who you are.

There was an article in *The New York Times* Sunday magazine section that was a study of mysticism in America. It turned out that two-fifths of the population of the United States at some point in their lives had a genuine transcendent mystical experience, an experience of breaking through who they thought they were. That's pretty impressive. That's more than forty million people. A sampling of those two-fifths showed that 85 percent of them said it was the most profound experience of their lives and they never wanted to have another one. Of course not, because it upset the apple cart.

You think you need to be who you think you are in order to keep the game going smoothly, to keep your ground. It's scary. It's like waking up out of a dream and not knowing where you are. Like when the lights go on in a movie theater and you're momentarily disoriented. Carl Jung, in *Memories, Dreams, Reflections,* said he went into these extraordinary realms, but he was so happy to come back to his wife and family and to reality. Still clinging to *this* as reality as opposed to *that.*

Who Are You?

Time goes by until one day you're ready to recognize you are here on earth as a soul who has taken birth in order to work through the attachments and clingings within yourself that keep you identified with your separateness. This allows you, once again, to become one with the One, or return to the Source, or to know your true self. When that recognition is deep enough, the whole meaning of your life changes.

You notice that you were busy being separate. At the moment of death, because you were totally identified with your separateness, you said, "I don't want to die. Stop the world, I don't want to get off. Doctors, save me! Implant, transplant, do whatever you have to do, but keep me alive. I don't want to die because death is the end of it all." If you are a philosophical materialist, you are your body, and if the body goes, you ain't. You're dead. Dead dead, not spiritual-dead dead. Then a voice says to you, "Welcome." I guess I didn't die if I'm still hearing somebody talk to me! The voice says, "Oh no, you did die." And you freak because it's so discrepant from who you thought you were. You go into total confusion, which is often called "purgatory," and you hang in there until you are processed, reeducated, programmed, and sent back.

Now you know you aren't who you thought you were, but you're not that far along in your spiritual work, so when death comes again, you say, "No, I don't want to die. *RamRamRam*, God, Christ, I don't want to die." There you are again, dead dead, and a voice says, "Welcome." And you say, "I guess I didn't die." And the voice says, "You did die." You pause for a moment. Suddenly everything you were trying to believe all your life turned out to be true. Far out!

You see your whole trip at that moment. You see how much work you've done in all your incarnations. You become a relatively conscious participant in the dance between incarnations. You see what work you have to do. What you are in this moment is another opportunity. It's another set of experiences. It's more grist for the mill for your soul to awaken to its true identity.

Awakening

When you understand this, then the meaning of your entire life changes because from then on everything in your life becomes a vehicle for awakening. It isn't only going to a lecture or meditating. It becomes all of it. You see that the game is exquisitely designed to provide you with the opportunities you need to burn out the ways in which you are clinging and lead you deeper into love.

As Buddha pointed out, it is the clinging that causes the suffering. It isn't living life that causes suffering. If you cling to health as your body decays and you can't acknowledge the decay—suffering. If you cling to the desire to be rich and you're poor—suffering. If you cling to having hair and you go bald—suffering. But it is what it is: the recognition that the meaning of an incarnation is to provide a set of experiences for the soul to awaken to its true self.

An incarnation is an opportunity, a set of choices that allow humanity to move into harmony with the will of God or away from it. It is a set of choices that allow you to return to God, which is the Source, which is the undifferentiated space, which is the Garden of Eden, which is home, which is love, which is who you turn out to be.

That's who you are. That's what you're doing here.

A thousand times, you will get lost again. You will forget what you're doing. You'll get lost into your "mellow-drama." You will get lost into the absolute reality of the illusion. The reason that this level seems so real all the time is because of your attachment to your senses and to your thoughts, to your smelling, tasting, hearing, touching, feeling, and knowing. You are very attached to the particular channel on TV to which you are tuned. "Illusion" isn't quite the right word, because this plane is as real as that plane, as that plane, as that plane. They are all relatively real. When you're in them, they're real. If you have to go to the bathroom, it's real. But many of you have transcended one level of reality and experienced another level of reality, and in that other level of reality, what seemed real doesn't seem real anymore.

The "Whole" Journey

The process is one of slowly awakening birth after birth or within a birth—the process of becoming more and more conscious of your predicament and less and less attached to this or that, to samsara or nirvana, to illusion or enlightenment.

And what is the process of liberation? Liberation means being liberated from the clinging to any single reality as *the* reality. Here we are, nowhere to stand.

If you are hearing my words now and forgetting to rise in your being and tune in to your soul, you are attached to the level of reality that is fed by your intellect. To some of you, these words are like *bzzz*, background noise, and you and I are moving higher and higher in a space of more and more clarity and quietness and openness and spaciousness. A liberated being is rising spiritually, heart open in love, totally aware at the level of the intellect, physically aware of their body and where they are sitting and of all their pains and aches and pleasures—all of it at the same time. Not clinging to this or that, not spacing out, not coming down.

Going up and coming down is not liberation; it's a roller coaster.

You spend lifetimes trying to get high in order to remember what it is you keep forgetting. Eventually, you don't forget very often, and then you are eager to get on with it. When you are eager to get on with it, you are less attached to your highs, for your highs and lows are all grist for the mill. Your highs teach you about other planes of reality. Your lows teach you about what's keeping you stuck in this particular reality.

Human Suffering

The object of the dance of enlightenment, of coming to God, is not to realize God and forget humanity. The formless and the form are two different faces of God. If you deny your incarnation in order to go to God, you don't know God fully. If you want perfection in your spiritual journey, you must both honor your incarnation and become totally free of it. You must both look up and recognize that beyond form lies formlessness, and that even within form lies the perfection of the design of things, the natural law, the Tao, the way of things.

You must understand the issue of social responsibility. Before you looked up, you were only looking down and out, and all you saw everywhere was suffering. All forms have suffering inherent within them because they are in time and space, subject to change and decay. It is just the way of things. Your heart bled for that suffering, and sometimes it was unbearable and you had to harden your heart because you couldn't bear the suffering. You looked up, or you went inside, and you started to experience deeper peace and higher consciousness. You felt the perfection of the universe, and in that clarity, all of the horror and the suffering fell into place, and you were up in the heights of the Himalayas dancing in the pure white snow.

But if you're going on the whole journey, then you must look down again. And when you look down, you see that there is blood upon the snow. There is the bleeding heart of Jesus. There is the suffering of all sentient beings. It is a strong and conscious and clear and liberated being who can simultaneously look down and experience unbearable compassion and, at the same moment, look up and see the exquisiteness of the perfection. Such a being is in a position to liberate other beings from suffering. Every act that is performed by such a being in relation to another human being creates the optimum conditions for that other being to be liberated from the attachment to their own suffering.

If you are hungry and I feed you, I am feeding your belly. But if I am attached to being the giver of the food, that creates a reality in which you are only the receiver of the food. If, however, I am giving you the food but, at the same moment, I am in a space in which there is no giving and no receiving, then this is merely the particular round of the melodrama we are playing out together.

Now we are becoming conscious. Now we are moving toward liberation. Now we are getting less lost in the emotionality of the dance. Now we can look about ourselves in this incarnation and see what our capabilities are as incarnated beings to end suffering. We can accept our dharma, our way, and do it as a vehicle for remaining in the perfection of the will of God.

Your Choice

Ultimately, the work is to open yourself to all the forms of the universe, of the universes, whether those forms be on the physical plane, the astral plane, the causal plane. Open yourself to them, acknowledge them, honor them, and go beyond them.

You have a choice. The pull from God, the pull of the formless to merge back into the formless and to leave behind your body and your personality and all of your stuff, is incredible. No blame either way. God is not in time so there's no rush about this game. You're all going to get enlightened sooner or later.

But a few beings push against God to stay in form in order to relieve the suffering of others. That is the sacrificial lamb. That is to leave the father to become the son; that was the sacrifice of Jesus the Christ, not the crucifixion. That's nothing for a liberated being. Taking on the suffering, the karma of others, that's great joy for a liberated being. Bleeding, pain, death, nothing, nothing. Even the statement "Father, why have you forsaken me?" can be understood as "Father, why do you glorify me? Why is the game going to turn out that everybody's going to worship me instead of remembering you?"

At this moment you are a being who hears what I'm saying, not because I'm saying it but because you hear it in your heart and know that it resonates in truth within yourself. There is no way you can go back. The hook is planted. The awakening is happening. It is irrevocable. You can no longer get totally lost in the illusion. You may make believe you are, you may try to be. You may wish this whole trip would go away and you could say it's just another trip, but it won't do that.

Unfortunately, you're hooked, and it won't be over until you can sit down and make your body firm, and draw in a breath, and let out that breath, and take in no further breath. The body will become stiff and the heartbeat will become quiet and you will leave the body and your soul will rise, leaving behind each of your bodies, all of the astral melodramas of the psychic planes, leaving behind the masters and the gurus and the methods, and you will come into the presence of God, into the unconditional love of God, and the last boundaries of separateness will start to disappear.

Chapter 6

From Head to Heart

Ram Dass spoke often of the connection and the divergence of the head and the heart and how each plays a part in our feeling of separateness and in becoming whole. The head and the heart each has its own perspective, its own way of seeing the world and one's inner being. The head, with its mighty intellect, acts as a shield for our separateness. The heart has the ability to break down all barriers, even the boundaries we need to live in the world. Together, they have a combined power that brings about true compassion for suffering.

In this chapter are some of the many ways in which Ram Dass works with bringing the head and the heart into balance with each other, into a harmony that leads to more love and the resolution of fear.

All of the ways in which we are separate are at some level rooted in fear, and one way of characterizing the difference between head and heart is the dialogue between fear and love. The minute you cultivate that part of you that is connected, that is part of the web of things in which we are *us*, then another quality comes into human relationships: you recognize the quality of love, of coming into love with people.

I was leading a course in New York City at Saint John the Divine in which everybody, including me, was required to volunteer either in a soup kitchen or a shelter or a political action around homelessness, and keep a diary of their experiences. Then we had an open microphone. A woman got up and said, "Every day I leave my apartment in Manhattan and I go to the corner to get the bus or go to the grocery. For the past eight months, there's been this man standing on the corner with a paper cup with some coins in it, jiggling the cup. I give him a little money now and then." She gave kind of a sheepish smile and said, "Actually, he's been there so long that I've worked out a budget of $2.50 a week. But as a result of taking this course, I realized I never really looked at him. I never acknowledged him as a human being. I realized that I was afraid."

So we started to talk about what she was afraid of. She wasn't afraid she was going to be sexually assaulted. She wasn't afraid her purse was going to be stolen. Finally she said, "I'm afraid that if I open my heart to him, he'll end up in my living room."

Does that resonate in you at all? Does it resonate in you that how you deal with the stuff of the world is rooted in fear that you will lose your boundaries? It's like I can't look at the suffering because it's too vast and it will overwhelm me, so I'll look away.

Look at the way the intuitive heart works. If you're really in love—I'm not talking about being attached to someone or romantic love; I'm talking about being in the space of love with another human being—your joy is in their joy. You need something? Take my car, take my credit card, take my life. Go ahead. I love you. You do what makes you happy. On the other hand, our fearful mind is constantly saying to the heart, "Now wait a minute. You can't give everything away. What about your health insurance?" The mind is continually setting boundaries. This is me, this is not me, this is good, this is bad. The mind is constantly judging. The heart is not judging; the heart is opening, so that the mind is actually afraid of the heart.

It's an interesting dialogue between the mind and the heart, because the mind is always protecting you as a separate entity while the heart is always saying, "What boundaries? You and I are *us*; there's no *them*." So the interesting question is, When and under what conditions can you meet people in such a way that you can keep your heart open without giving up your discriminative wisdom about how to be with another person?

What this woman on the street with the homeless man was saying is "I am afraid if I look at this human being and acknowledge his existence, my heart will open and it will know no boundaries." It seems to me that's a failure to understand that our harmonious state isn't the tyranny of the heart over the mind or the tyranny of the mind over the heart. It isn't the tyranny of our separateness over the way we are a unit or unity, nor is it the tyranny of our unity over the uniqueness that each of us possesses.

It's a perfect balancing.

The Mind Thinks/The Heart Feels

The heart is the other side of the mind, which is the computer central for running you as a separate entity. The mind thinks about things, thinks about objects. It's the computer for your space suit, for your body and your personality, and it's saying, "*Danger*, pull back. Be careful of that person."

You think the enemy is outside, but actually the enemy isn't outside. The mind's enemy is the heart. When you trip and fall into love, what wouldn't you do for your beloved? Let me get you breakfast, a flower. What do you want? For the beloved, you would do anything. That's what the mind's afraid of. So there's this interesting dialogue going on between this innate quality of compassion in us and the mind, which veils it and cuts it off.

If you're a doctor or nurse, you become what's called "professionally warm," which is when your emotions are in the service of your intellect. Your intellect says, "Isn't that too bad." You say, "Oh, I feel terrible," and you do, but you don't really let it in because you've got to save your heart for the grandchildren or for your husband or for when you get home.

The heart is too unruly. The heart doesn't know boundaries; pure consciousness doesn't have boundaries. The discriminating mind decides that this is this and this is that, this is me and this is you. That's functional for keeping the separate entity going, but if that's all you think you are, you feel very vulnerable and tiny because it's a big game. So the mind is continuously responding. Its juice is fear. It's constantly saying, "That's a tree, that's a car." It's always having to define everything to make sure it's all safe. To protect ourselves, the mind says, "Leave it to me." We start to get identified with our thoughts of who we are, which is our space suit. Then, when we are identified with our space suit, all we see are other space suits and we lose the fact that the person we're with is really *us*.

But you and I are beginning to realize that isn't exactly right. It's much more interesting than that. I've spent all these years trying to become holy or divine or something, and I met this colleague from Harvard and after about fifteen minutes he said, "You know, Dick, you haven't changed a bit." But the fact is that I have changed. One of the things that's changed is the quality of my heart because I'm learning how to keep my heart open.

I'm learning to do that by noticing what closes my heart, what armors my heart. When my mind clicks in and takes over, it puts an armoring around my heart to protect me. The armoring of the mind around the heart is interesting. It's doing two things at once. It's keeping spears and arrows from getting in and hurting your heart, but it's also keeping your heart from overwhelming your ego because your heart will give away everything.

The mind is saying, "Wait a minute, wait a minute, you've got to think about tomorrow." The heart knows the quality of love. It flows outward. The heart knows the part of you that is not vulnerable. The mind is only an instrument to protect that part of you which is vulnerable. There's the trap right there. Are you vulnerable, or aren't you? Christ said, "Look, I took a human birth just like you. I'll show you we are not vulnerable. Look, what are they going to do? They're going to laugh at me.

You think it's hurting me? I'm here. They're going to scorn me. Look, they're going to nail me up. I'll drop back in three days and I'll show you that isn't who I am either."

See, when you are in your mind and you're separate and you're looking at other people, they're separate and they're people to be dealt with and you relate to them in terms of power and need and your personality. The minute you come up for air, you look around and see your sister and your brother, you see yourself. You see there's only one of us appearing to be the many.

What happened to most of us was that we tasted that unity, which started to feed us. Our hearts were open and getting fed, like heart-to-heart resuscitation feeding the juices into the being so you don't burn out and dry up. When people are only in their minds, they're very dry, brittle, cynical, frightened, tight people. When you first realize how caught you are in your own mind, very often you try to push it violently away, which is the renunciation path. It's like this is all a crock and I'm going to the Himalayas. I'm going to go into a cave and stay away from the cities. But that is the newness of realizing there are other realities; you push against one to get to another one. After a while you realize that if you are pushing against anything, you may be getting high but you're not getting free. Being free means you're not standing anywhere or you are standing everywhere, meaning you are both the One and the many.

Balancing Head and Heart

We try to feel our way into the balance of the mind and the heart, but it involves all of us. It involves this quality of consciousness that we share together because you and I are like family. It's funny how in our zeal to be independent and our misunderstanding of what freedom means, we have taken the term "family" and made it almost into an obligation. Yet the quality of the feelings that family represents is the sustenance that we need, that nourishes us.

Taking care of my father as he died was one of the deepest feelings I have received in this lifetime. Mother Teresa, as she picks up a leper in the streets of Calcutta, says that she is serving Christ in all his "distressing disguises" and she serves God through serving that person. We look at her and say, "How courageous." But it's not courage; it's grace. How graceful to be able to feel safe enough to look at people with love and to look at people as poignant instead of with anger and separation when their minds get out of balance with their hearts.

If you quiet down enough, you can listen to hear your unique part in the whole dance. As you quiet down and get less busy being somebody, you hear more because you are more. You start to expand in awareness until you are all of it. Then you start to function from intuitive wisdom, not from intellectual knowledge. Knowledge is wonderful and it's great to develop the skill of the mind; it's a great servant, but a lousy master.

We have an inner-balance problem between our minds and our hearts. We have an outer-balance problem that will allow us to honor our relationships to the ecosystems in which we dwell—people, species, earth, cosmology. We cultivate the quality of attentive, appreciative listening. We quiet our minds so we can hear more clearly. The Tao says truth waits for "eyes unclouded by longing." As long as you want something, you only see the outward container. But if you don't want anything and you think the world might blow up (and wouldn't that be interesting), why would you do anything to have the world not blow up? Because you're also a human and that's what you as a human would do. You're also an individual and part of the truth of your incarnation is the preservation of you and your children and your children's children to the seventh and the seven thousandth generation.

We have two things to deal with—a quiet mind and an open heart. If you only have a quiet mind, you may see the laws of karma. You may see the plan of the universe. You may see the higher wisdom. You may understand it all, but you lose your ground. You become like a god on earth. But you did take an incarnation. You are in a human body. And to be in a human body means to realize that you are part of humanity and have all the human feelings that generate pity, sadness, empathy, horror, beauty, joy. To keep that balance is what the nature of compassion is about. Compassion keeps the heart open so that you are feeling all the suffering of all the beings around you, which is really hard to do. And at the same moment, you keep the appreciation of the way it's all dharmic law unfolding. As Maharajji kept saying to me, "Ram Dass, don't you see it's all perfect?"

The head shows you the perfection, which includes the suffering. Suffering burns out our stuff and awakens us. You'd never lay it on somebody else, but when it's there, you see how it's working on them. That's the beauty of the mind. The mind can plumb the depths of the wisdom of the universe and appreciate the exquisite way in which it all works. But if you stay up there, you get so cold.

These talks are such an exercise for me because they're a blend of head and heart. If I get too far one way or the other, the whole thing comes unglued. It doesn't do what it can do. But when there's a nice balance of head and heart, it's like swimming in ambrosia. I don't yet have much control over it. Sometimes we hit it and sometimes we don't because my mind is such fun to play with, and to play with a lot of other people is such fun. There are always these people that want to go on mind trips, but without the heart they're kind of harsh.

The problem with the heart is, if you get into that and leave the mind behind, everything becomes kind of a Slurpee. It's all universal oneness in a glop and you lose your zip code. If I go too far the other way, then there are people in the audience that say, "See? That's what comes from taking too much acid." I could go around the country being a piece of datum about people that took hundreds and hundreds of trips and demonstrate what happened to their brains. And you paid to hear me. Can you imagine that?

When I was teaching hatha yoga, somebody would say they'd like to fast. "Oh, yogini," I'd say, "are you healthy?"

And they say, "Yes. I'd like to fast four days."

I say, "No, fast nine."

"Nine days? What can I take?"

"Well, take warm water or lemon and water or tea."

So they look courageous and they go out to fast for nine days. They come in after seven days and say, "I haven't eaten in seven days." There's a little bit of ego stuff in there. Okay, they haven't eaten in seven days. So you kind of feed that. You say, "Pretty good, you're doing fine. Only two more days to go."

Then you walk out in the street and somebody comes up and says, "Hey, man, got a quarter? Man, I haven't eaten in seven days."

"Good, you're doing fine. Two more days and you'll be free."

You can feel exactly the whole issue right there. They are both doing the same thing. They're both suffering. For one of them, the suffering is grace. For the other, the suffering is suffering. If your job is to relieve suffering, to the first one you say, "You're doing fine with seven days, maybe try seven more." With the other one you say, "Here's a quarter."

From Head to Heart

Most people identify with their thoughts. A thought comes along in the river of thoughts: "Oh, I want that. I want that." Or maybe it's a negative thought: "This is uncomfortable. Yeah, this is uncomfortable." Most people are in their heads and they're so far in their heads that they don't realize that their heart is calling. Guru, God, and self call out to each of us. Inside. Instead of looking outside, try looking inside. You'll find the treasure of yourself inside.

In our hearts, in our spiritual hearts, we witness our thoughts. Thoughts come and go, but we don't identify with them. Some people refer to this spiritual heart as the soul; it witnesses not only our thoughts and the senses, but also our incarnations, our lives. Most people don't know the real self. Most people don't know that *awareness is in the heart*. Awareness, what your eyes see; awareness, what your ears hear; awareness, what your skin feels; awareness, what your mind spews forth as thoughts.

We try to learn how to move our identification from up in the head to here in the heart. Then, when you have soul perception, the world is a different place. When I was up here in my head, I was full of insecurity; here in the heart, I was full of love. I couldn't believe it. I believed Maharajji was full of love, but me? Full of love? It got so that I saw everything around as lovable. You're lovable. I'm lovable. This chair is lovable. The tent is lovable. I start to love my environment and it brings me closer to my environment. I go out to a tree and I don't look at it as just a tree—that's an external thing. I look at it with loving eyes and I meld with it. I meld with the whole universe.

Up here in the head, we have who we think we are. Little individuals. When we identify with the individual, you know what we get? We get fear because everything is big; the wind and all the elements and politics and everything . . . everything is big. But we can get back into our hearts. We can identify with the whole cosmos. I am my soul. My soul is not under time and space. My soul is infinite. It's infinite. The body is time and space. But who I am inside, no, no.

This incarnation, from birth to death, is one of a series of incarnations your soul takes from the One to the One. This incarnation is your karma because the karma of your soul gave you this incarnation. It gave you this body, it gave you these parents, this culture, these friends, these attitudes. All of this stuff is your karma. You think you are this body. You think you had this mother and father. You think that the world is real. All of its wars and stuff like that. Oh, boy. But you come down into the heart, the soul. Well, look at this, another incarnation. The incarnation has an ego. The ego says, "Oh, I'm afraid of death." But the soul says, "It's just another death."

So we are here to get into our souls and see our egos as thoughts. This is the thought of who I am. This is who I really am. Hello, souls.

Chapter 7

From Role to Soul

The journey to wholeness is not only from head to heart but also from role to soul. The question is one of identification. Who am I if I'm not a parent and grandparent, a writer, an American? Who are you when all the labels fall away? What happens when we are stripped of our roles? Who are we then? Ram Dass refers to this as "becoming nobody" rather than as our perceived vision of ourselves as "somebody."

Ram Dass shows us what it means to become our souls instead of our roles.

I work about half of my time with people who have AIDS or cancer as they're dying. I hold them as they're dying and I talk with them. I'm with them. When I meet such a being, they have a certain symbolic value in my world as a dying person with AIDS and I have a certain symbolic value to them—I am a person who has come to help them die. If we stay at that level, if I stay in my role and they stay in their role, we stay separated from one another. The relationship can be very kind, but it doesn't feed either one of us. People who help other human beings but stay in their role of helper, they ultimately burn out. They burn out because they're not being fed by the interaction.

I went to visit a friend of mine who had AIDS. He had pneumocystis and my heart was breaking for him. I knew his career was just coming together and how painful this was for his ego, for his personality. My personality was screaming with pain for his personality and we cried together. But my soul was saying to his soul, or my awareness was saying to his awareness, "Hi, you in there? I'm in here. Well, this is a heavy one. See if you can stay conscious through this one. You still here, or did you get lost into being somebody with AIDS?"

I realized at some point that what was required was that I had to open my heart to this person and see behind the roles we were both caught in, see beyond identifying this being with his AIDS. I am trapping him into being somebody with AIDS, but beyond that he's a being. When I can find the place in myself that is my being, not the person who is helping someone with AIDS but just a being, then I can meet him as being to being. The minute we do that, our hearts are open to one another and then the AIDS and the helping start to become ground instead of figure. Suddenly we are both being fed by the love of our mutual presence. Once you understand the way in which relationships are going to feed you, you develop the capacity to not get caught in the symbolic identity of each other.

What do I mean by "symbolic identity"? All the identities of father, son, mother, daughter, person with AIDS, person who helps, beautiful, ugly, old, young. I was on the funicular one day and Helmut Schmidt, the chancellor of West Germany, was standing next to me. I was aware of how powerful his symbolic identity was, which made it very hard for me to see him as another person on the cable car with me. I couldn't let go of his symbolic power. In another example, I've hung out with models, women who are culturally defined as very beautiful and appear in *Harper's Bazaar* and *Vogue* and so on. When I spend time with them as human beings, I experience the incredible isolation they feel because their symbolic value is so powerful that nobody can be behind it with them. It's so powerful it intervenes in all relationships.

Our job continually is to get out of our roles. If we get caught in them, we get reactive. Son does something, it elicits fatherness; father does something, it elicits son-ness, and we keep each other as objects. Can we meet behind father- and son-ness? Are you here? I'm here. We're fellow human beings. Well, what will we do today? I'll tell you what—I'll be your father. Okay, I'll be the son.

You say, "But I really am his father." Well, you are and you aren't. You happen to, at this moment in time and space, be in a biological relationship as the "father" to this other human being that is labeled as your "son." But behind that, you are a being and he is a being and you have to listen to that being carefully because that being has their own story. They have their own genetics, they have their own karmic predicament, as it is called in the East. It's extremely hard to do that, because if you're identified with father-ness, you need your son to be a certain way in order for you to be a good father.

Somebody Training

The way I see it is we are shared awareness. You and I incarnated on this trip and came into this awareness. Once we were in form, our form interacted with other forms. Usually the way I say it is we went into *somebody* training. I came in to awareness and then slowly I was taught I'm Richard. You were taught you're somebody else, but I was Richard. I was the template on which my parents printed my identity because I was who they thought I was, since their consciousness was defining my reality, plus my genetics, my karma, and a few other little variables. So I went into somebody training and I became very much of a somebody.

Everybody's in somebody training. Weren't you trained to be somebody? I was. And I thought it was real. That was what was so far-out—everyone thought it was real. We get so well socialized into being somebody that the problem is we get trapped in our somebody-ness. Our parents thought they were somebody and they were certainly going to train somebody. They don't train nobody. So you become somebody. You really know who you are. You've got diplomas. People say, "She's really somebody!" I work a lot with nobody in my own mind, and Wavy Gravy [a peace activist involved with the Seva Foundation] is very helpful to me with his Nobody for President campaign. He has all these slogans, like "Nobody can solve our economic problems." His best one is "Nobody cares." See, to me that's a statement of compassion. Nobody cares. I'd say that's the advanced course.

Once I was a somebody, I was no longer everything; once I was no longer everything, I'll tell you, I felt a little separate. I felt a little hungry and I felt a little cold and a little frightened because I was very little and the forces in the universe were very big, starting with my mother, let alone cyclones, tornadoes, and other natural phenomena. Because I felt so little, the world of power became real to me. How do I keep enough power to survive as a separate entity? And I developed very strong needs and desires as a separate entity. I need this. I want this. So I grew up being somebody.

Then in 1961, when I took mushrooms from the kind hand of Timothy Leary, I recognized that who I thought I was was a hype. I'd been had. What I was was much more interesting than that. In fact, everybody's in drag, busy being somebody. The minute I tasted that, my whole agenda in life changed. It changed so dramatically that I got thrown out of Harvard.

I had this peculiar moment of standing in front of the television and the radio business at my moment of glory when I had been thrown out of Harvard, when all these guys looked at me and I was the bad guy and I was the loser and I was the one who was going to go down in ignominy. It's like somebody who's fought Muhammad Ali and lost for the third time, and he's going to end up as a training instructor in a gym on the Lower East Side. They're saying a final goodbye. He lost the hundred-million-dollar purse and he's going down and it's all horrible.

I remember standing there and seeing that look in all of their eyes while this thing happened inside of me, which was so valid—I was suddenly free of this incredible cultural burden of being somebody who I didn't think I was anymore. In my rational mind, I was enough of a psychologist that I was saying to myself, "Look, when you think one reality and everybody else thinks another, you know you are psychotic, baby." Isn't that what the game is? Because psychosis is consensus about reality. You need three psychiatrists to say you're crazy and you're crazy, even though they may be and you may not be.

My agenda had changed because I saw so clearly that if I am busy being a somebody, my actions keep perpetuating the separation between people. My somebody-ness reinforces everybody else's somebody-ness. That is very complicated because if you are busy being a helper, you demand that the other person is the helped. I really thought I was a therapist. Finally I realized that I could be a being in a room with another being and do what we need to do. If we need me to be a therapist, I will play therapist. You begin to appreciate that you can extricate yourself from your definitions of who you think you are. It doesn't mean you can't do all those things; you just can't identify with them. You can take them off and put them on.

Beyond the Role

The growth for each of us is to grow out of having to be identified with our social roles. We may be busy being doctor or patient or wife or mother or father or teacher or any of the trips in life, but behind it all, here we are. There's Ram Dass. He's charming and he's neurotic. He's delightful, he's playful, he's bald, he's got an older body. But here I am and here you are, and you have your trips as I have mine. I keep meeting people and they all think they're somebody. They think I think I'm somebody, but most of the time I'm not somebody. I am nobody. I appear like somebody to somebody who needs to find somebody. You need a therapist. Here I am. You need a lover? Here I am. I'm everything and I'm nothing. Why do I have to be something? Is there a law?

I do Ram Dass out there. I'm still in here. I'm still loving awareness, but everybody wants Ram Dass from me. As long as you don't get too attached to the role, you can play it or not play it. It doesn't matter. But most of us have roles we are very wedded to and those are the ones you worry about because, when you are in that role, it takes over. Still, I am loving awareness. I am loving awareness, and my role is out there. You have to play the game if you're going to be a human being. The question is where you play that game from. And I think the place to play that from is your soul.

What is this "soul"? It is a unique entity that is part of the oneness, and, when the time is right, clothes itself in a personality and body to take birth on the physical human plane. This personality and body are much like space suits for dwelling on earth. Inevitably, in all but the rarest cases, within a few years the infant will become so much identified with its space suit that it loses its memory of its identity as a soul. Then we live our lives engaged in human vocations until our deaths, when we leave behind the space suit and once again remember our true selves as souls.

What happens when you are not identified with your somebody-ness? There's an incredibly beautiful woman saint, Anandamayi Ma, who died in the eighties in India. I've sat with groups of ten thousand to watch her, to hear her sing to God, or to feel her presence. It's called having darshan. She says:

> This body has lived with father, mother, husband, and all. This body has served the husband, so you may call it a wife. It has prepared dishes for all, so you may call it a cook. It has done all sorts of scrubbing and menial work, so you may call it a servant. But if you look at the thing from another standpoint, you will realize that this body has served none but God. For when I serve my father, mother, husband, and others, I simply considered them as different manifestations of the Almighty and served them as such. . . . I had but one ideal to serve all as God, to do everything for the sake of God.

You in There?

You go through life meeting people—lovers, friends, relatives, storekeepers, people on the street, protagonists. You either see the costume or you see the essence. It depends on which way you focus your eyes. You can see different degrees of essence depending on how you fine-tune. You start out seeing body and clothing. Then you tune in to personality. That's costume. There's a decent chap. Then you look behind that and you see a soul who thinks that they are a decent chap.

"Hello, soul, you in there?"

"Hello, leave me alone."

"I'm a decent chap. Aw, come on out and play."

Or you can shift your glance once more and then you see there's only one of it and it includes you. So it's God saying to God, "You in there?" It's the One talking of itself and it's you being a good chap. You can flick your consciousness and meet whomever you want all day long. It's all relative reality, whatever reality you think is real. There's nowhere to stand. Any place you think you're standing keeps dissolving away from you. It's another place to stand, another opinion, another attitude, another somebody doing something. It is like two actors on a stage, each costumed for their part.

If you go back far enough in consciousness, go back in relationships, you find the awareness that there is only one of you. I feel so much love for that being who is going through this process of incarnation that my heart opens wide because I recognize none other than myself. The one God, the one spirit, comes into all these forms. The art is to see through the individual differences, to honor them, to honor our incarnation and individual differences, but not get lost in the drama of them. So when you meet another being that you recognize:

"Are you in there? I'm in here."

"Far out! Well, I'm about to die of AIDS this time."

"Oh, didn't you do that last time?"

"No, last time . . ."

"Well, have a good journey!"

See how weird it is? There's nowhere to stand. We are God, we are souls, we are personalities, we are bodies. We are cellular structures. We are patterns of energy. We are a dance, a play. We are God in drag. What you meet are people who are coming up to you and saying, "I'm real. This is real." They are pulling to catch you. For them, it is so real that they are using you because their faith isn't strong enough. Because it isn't that real. They're using you to confirm the fact that they think it's real: "It's real, isn't it?"

I was staying at a motel, and around two in the morning I went to get change for a one-dollar bill for the Coke machine. The night attendant came out and he said, "Aren't you Ram Dass? Can I talk to you?" Okay. He said, "You know what? I read spiritual books, and I've really touched all of this, but I don't know how to manifest it. Here I am, a night clerk in this motel. That's it. I mean, is that enough? Aren't I blowing it? Shouldn't I be doing something more me?"

Can you hear the question? Well, the first answer is, it doesn't make any difference. To which he says, "Well, it makes a difference to me." To which I say, "Well, that is your problem." He's free to see that he is the creator of the situation he finds himself in, instead of just being the guy that's found himself in it. What form should the Buddha come in this time? Golden robes, aerial chariots, a scent of flowers? It might be as the night clerk in the motel. How about a motel night manager who likes to frequent bars and meet young ladies? "Come on now. God couldn't come in that form." Because you don't think so, you won't see it. Most people are so busy with their trips that God could be standing on the corner and everybody would walk right by seeing something different.

All you and I have to offer one another is what we are, not what we think we are. When I come out here, you're not really picking up on what I'm saying; you're picking up on what I am and either it's feeding a place in you or it isn't. Maybe tonight you are a motel night clerk and tomorrow you're not. Maybe ten years from now, you're still a night clerk in the motel. You ready? Can you allow for all possibilities? Can you allow for the fact that you are exactly where you are supposed to be and that the whole scene is going fine?

I was with this woman who was dying, and she said to me, "Ram Dass, please help me die. I'm so bored." I said, "Well, Jean, that's because you're busy dying all the time. I mean, it's one scenario. You don't have to do it full-time. Couldn't you die like five minutes an hour? The rest of the time, let your body die while you hang out, listen to the birds and stuff. You don't have to be busy dying. It's a very draggy role to play all the time."

Any role is.

Do You See *Me*?

I've got the front page of a Seattle newspaper that shows a guy in prison, John Doe, a man they imprisoned but they can't figure out who he is. He had a dispatch case full of identities, but none of them were his. When asked who he was, he said, "You arrested me. It's your job to find out. I know who I am." The sergeant said John Doe has in effect foiled our system. It's the Nasrudin joke. Nasrudin is a kind of crazy meshugeneh saint. He goes in to cash a check and he looks like such a bum. The teller looks at the check and says, "Yeah, the check's fine, but, sir, can you identify yourself?" Nasrudin reaches into his pocket and pulls out a mirror and says, "Yep, that's me."

I was teaching a course in dying with Elisabeth Kübler-Ross. There was a thirty-four-year-old nurse there who had three children. She had had cancer since childhood and had undergone well over forty operations by this time, so she spent a lot of time in a hospital bed, as well as a nurse working in a hospital. She said, "What would you feel if you came to visit me in the hospital? What would you feel?"

People called out things—I would feel angry at God for doing this to you; I would feel pity; I would feel the pain of your situation—and the list went on and on. She said, "Notice in all of these you are busy responding to the fact that I am a thirty-four-year-old woman with three children who has cancer. Nobody was responding to me."

Can you hear that? Can you hear the difference between the role she was in and the identity of the being back in there? She said, "I felt tremendously isolated in that hospital, because nobody was with *me*; everybody was with their projection of the person who was sick in that way." Do you understand the issue? Because it's a really interesting one. When you are with people and you are both in your respective roles, you get trapped in the roles. The roles form an efficient way of being together, but they also separate you from each other. You end up seeing the other person as "Oh, that's Harry. He's always this way."

It's so bizarre in our human relationships, the way we enter into these conspiracies together. The fact of the matter is that you and I are a tremendously complex set of levels of reality. When you come down to breakfast every morning, you're a different person some mornings from who you are on other mornings. When you come into relationship with people you know, their expectations of who you are get you to conspire to enter into that level of reality with them. You push the rest of you aside. I'll make believe you are who you think you are, if you will make believe I am who I think I am. Well, that's efficient. I know her, she's Doris. I know him, he's Sam. Sam is Sam and

Doris is Doris. It's like cookie cutting when you cut the cookie and then push away all the dough around it. All the stuff that doesn't fit into my model of Doris- or Sam-ness becomes irrelevant. I'm only getting one little facet of who you are because my mind only lets in the well-shaped cookie and not the messy dough.

The interesting thing is what it is like to be with another human being where you don't impose models on each other of who everybody is all the time. Instead, you listen afresh to hear whom you're meeting and allow another person to change. You awaken and realize that the reality you thought was real, that defined who you were, is only another reality. You're beginning to understand that there are other realities as well and that you may be much more interesting than you thought you were. And that maybe the schlock, unworthy, inadequate, guilt-ridden overachiever that you were busy being isn't necessarily who you have to be for the rest of your life. You have a sense of a different being in yourself.

That is what happened to me with psychedelics in '61: I had a sense of my own existence quite independent of my social roles. Most people are very identified with their social role, and if not with their social role as mother or son or responsible citizen or as vamp, or as explorer of the future, or whatever social role you think of yourself in, most people are very identified with their bodies. I am forty-five, I am bald, I am a man. I can watch the things that change in my life. I can remember ten years ago when I let the hair grow very long on this side so I could comb it over here so I wouldn't look bald because I was busy being identified with the body. And then I began to notice when it didn't matter anymore. It stopped being that relevant.

When you sense that you are neither your social roles nor even your body, there are still many levels for confusion from then on, because the first thing you experience is you are a soul, an entity. Later, Buddha points out that that turns out to be a hype too. But for the moment, you break identification with your body and with your personality and with your sociology in order to become a spiritual entity. Then that spiritual entity has to do its work. That's the transformation that we're having.

The problem is that you are, at this point, simultaneously a spiritual entity, a psychological entity, and a physical entity, and you can't get rid of any of them quite yet. There's a horror show in that predicament. You get incredibly high in the spiritual sense and then suddenly your physical identity reasserts itself and there you are, a lusting animal. "That's not me," says the soul. And the body says, "You wanna bet?"

Dying into Your Roles

At this point, I have no idea who I am. I don't even care. It's like at some point I went into what you'd call "nobody training." Nobody special. I walk into the hall in the evenings and people come up to me and they say, "Hello, Ram Dass." When you're not somebody, how do you respond? Well, what you realize is if you don't care, you let the projections of other people form you. Ram Dass? Yes. It's different from "Hi, Dick." You can feel those roles changing. When you don't care who you are, you start to feel the way in which other people's minds keep defining reality.

My father was dying and was at the stage where all he had to do to keep his game going on earth was to swallow and breathe. We had taken over everything else, but we weren't going to do those two functions for him. That was up to him. If he didn't want to swallow food, we weren't going to feed him intravenously, and if he wasn't going to breathe, we weren't going to get respirators. We knew how to stick stuff in so he could get stuff out and it all worked fine—a long intestinal tract surrounded by a body. We were surrounding him with love and massages. He was lying there and he'd smile every now and then. He was like the Buddha.

One of my brothers would come, and he had had a hard time with my father in life and was still sort of angry. He'd say, "Hi, Dad." And Dad would look at him. My brother would walk out of the room and say, "He hasn't changed a bit; he won't even speak to me." Then my aunt came, my father's little sister who loved and worshipped my father. She sat down by the bed and took his hand and said, "Hello, George." He looked at her, just kept looking, and she says, "Oh my God, I can hardly stand it. He isn't who he used to be. Where is my Georgie?"

Can you hear all this? Here's my brother saying, "The bastard hasn't changed a bit." Here is my aunt saying, "Oh my God, he's not here anymore." They're both attached to the model of who they thought he was. What is he? He's the Buddha lying there. Why bum rap him for what he did before? Who he is now is much groovier than whoever he was before. I'm in ecstasy taking care of whatever form of God this is.

I realized that my humanity was made up of webs of relationships. My incarnation as a separate entity, that was the genetic one. That was my family. There were sexual identities, religious identities, all kinds of clubs, memberships, nation-states, ecosystems. I had a part to play in all of it. I've been given parts to play. Wow, I'll have to learn my lines.

When you hear your way into the web of it all and then somebody has needs, that's part of your definition of yourself. It's not something you as an individual say, "I think I'll do it." It's the part of you that's like a tree or river. I went at it as an exercise in spirituality, saying, "Well, I'll try being a member of the family and I'll go and take care of my dear old dad." I milked it. Look, I take care of my father. I used it as much as I could and my father provided me with infinitely good material for lectures. Then pretty soon it was just taking care of Dad. It felt harmonious to do.

At that moment, I began to be fed by the process. I began to feel at home in my familial identity. It's like you die into your role. You die into your unique karma. You don't end up being the Buddha or Christ. You end up being you. That balance is awfully interesting and very profound.

In all the years that I was a psychotherapist, psychologist, clinician, professor, drug taker, guru follower, meditator, doer of spiritual practices, yogi, all this stuff, I have never gotten rid of one neurosis, not one. I mean, you'd think by atrophy alone some would've gone. They're all still absolutely present. I can find every one of them. But instead of being these huge monsters that come and take me over, like lust, I'm sitting here very much at peace, and lust comes in and it goes, "Won't you come up and see my holy pictures?" Lust would use anything. It was using me mercilessly. Now, instead of it being this huge monster, it's just a little thought. Hello, sexual perversity. Haven't seen you in weeks. Come on in.

My personality is a style. It's a form to manifest in. You've got to be somebody. Just don't take it too seriously. The soul, you can go burrow into it. First you will have the individual soul, my soul. And as you burrow into it, you get to *the* soul—the still, small voice of God. The guru is in there. That oversoul is what unites us. When you identify with the soul, you have love inside, compassion inside, wisdom inside. Not knowledge that you get outside, but wisdom inside. Peace. I love people yelling for peace. All they have to do is go inside. Go inside. And joy, joy, joy. In yourself is joy. It's what we found when we were in the presence of Maharajji in India. He was joyful. He was compassionate. He was peaceful and he was loving.

From Role to Soul

I'm on the board of an organization called the Seva Foundation. A group of us came together in 1979 to share our common desire to help relieve suffering in the world. We realized that we were very imperfect instruments, so the criteria we set was that we would join together in a service to relieve suffering but we would also use it as a way for us to grow, to become freer and thus become better instruments of service. And we would have fun doing it. The first project that we took on was preventable and curable blindness, and the country of Nepal invited us in.

We had a rotating chairman of the board, and my turn came at a time when we were about to build one of our hospitals in Nepal. I suddenly found myself in Nepal, because we're a hands-on board. I was meeting with the minister of health in Nepal, who works for the king. It's a real monarchy. I mean, the king can say "Off with your head," and that's it. By that time, I had left academia and I had been a practicing communal hippie for a long time. Now here I was in my blue blazer and my red tie and I was really going to be *somebody* as a representative of the Seva Foundation. I had to keep my act together and I had to make sure we got what we needed from the government. The minister of health also had a wish list, because when you're the third-poorest country in the world and you meet somebody who is the head of a foundation from America, it's like meeting Santa Claus. From my point of view, I needed him to let go of certain bureaucratic restrictions, so I came in with my wish list; he came in with his own wish list.

We sit down, we have tea. I have my entourage, he has his entourage. I am very nervous because I'm going to have to be very strong in this situation. I'm busy being chairman of the board and busy seeing him—he's got his Nepali dress on—as the minister of health. In passing I happen to look into his eyes. And as I look into his eyes, what I experience is that somebody is looking back at me. He's right there. In effect, he is saying hello. It's as if you have a television receiver with a control dial right here by your eyes. I was tuned to the channel where we were social roles, and he was tuned to another channel where he was a fellow being looking out at me. "Are you there? I'm here." Far out.

What happened at that moment was that the plane of reality shifted for us and I saw the entire dialogue around hospital and bargaining and winning and losing in the same way as I would play a game of Monopoly. Chairman of the board became the thimble and minister of health became the top hat. We were bargaining Marvin Gardens for Park Place. We understood that we had come together to play a game, a game of life really, but the key point is we were meeting behind the game. Once we recognized that, we started to go at our bargaining.

We each fought very fiercely for what we wanted, but the profound impact of that meta meeting behind the level at which we were opponents was that the more we bargained, the more we began to appreciate each other and the closer we became as friends. By the end of it, we were in the space of love together.

Chapter 8

Be Here Now

Ram Dass's book Be Here Now *has been with us for over fifty years. That's a lot of present moments that have come and gone, although it is still where we are trying to go. Ram Dass went from* Be Here Now *to* Still Here, *to eventually not being here on earth at all but feeling as present as ever.*

Time is tricky, a devilish construct that attempts to order our lives into a past and a future, never stopping for long in the present. Yet here we are in this present moment—beings who are becoming more aware of ourselves as souls, beings who are embracing the journey from head to heart, beings who are learning to go beyond our experience of separation and are heading toward wholeness. How do we let go of who we were in the past? How do we not get lost in fears or fantasies of who we will be in the future? What does it mean to be here now?

"Be here now" was the principle lesson Ram Dass learned on his pilgrimage with Bhagavan Das in 1967 that led to his first meeting with Maharajji. In Being Ram Dass, *he described it like this:*

> *At first it was an adventure, and the spartan conditions didn't bother me. But it was very hot, and as the days went by, I needed to distract myself from the blisters and bad food. I tried to entertain myself*

by narrating my past exploits to Bhagavan Das. I thought he would be amused, but he was completely uninterested. When I told my stories, he simply replied, "Just be here now." I was thrown back into myself. Just be. Here. Now.

"Be here now" is the ultimate wisdom. Almost all spiritual practices are designed to bring you into the moment. When you're doing Tai Chi, at first you are thinking about it, but after a while, each movement is a fixed moment in which you are right where that movement is. In a way, when Tai Chi's working, you die into it and then the moment is just the movement of the hand at that point.

Similarly, in devotional practice, when you love, you start with the romantic dualistic "I love you"; it's self-conscious love, aware that you are loving. As the love starts to intensify, that self-consciousness disappears and there is the fullness of the state of love. Love brings you into the present moment. When we are together in love, there is the fullness of the moment. You can feel it when you fall in love with somebody, that the falling has all the drama around it, but in the state of being in love with a person, you can feel the timelessness of the moment.

As you open the heart by quieting the mind, you dwell more and more fully in *this moment* because the mind is what has past and future. The mind is what's going and coming. You dwell in this moment, but what has this moment got in it? In this moment, am I sad? Well, at this moment there is a baby dying, one every forty-five seconds from malnutrition in this world while our grain silos are overflowing. Am I sad? Yes, I'm sad. Am I happy? Yeah. At this moment, a new baby is coming out into the world. The first cry, the joy of the family, the creation, another soul has come through in order to do its work. The beauty and the preciousness of that. Am I happy? Sure. Can I be sad and happy at the same moment? If I can't be, I'm not in the moment. To be in the moment means to embrace it all . . . to embrace it all.

The fullness of "be here now" has the future and the past in it. People think that being here now means you're not being responsible. But all the past and the future—everything you always were and all of your commitments for the future—are in this moment. The fullness of this moment includes everything. It doesn't exclude past and future. All we are dealing with is the human mind that takes us into time and into space and takes us away from the fullness of the moment.

How Do You Get Here Now?

In Vipassana, insight meditation, you keep extricating yourself from identification with thoughts about past and future by noting them and then coming back to the present moment and the breath. The reason the breath is so good to work with is it's always around; it's right there and it's easy. You don't have to carry it with you. It's there in supermarkets, everywhere. There's always breath.

I do that all the time. I'm in traffic and somebody's cut me off. I feel the thought forms arising and I start to follow my breath as I'm driving. I can feel that at first I'm busy with my anger and busy with my driving. After a little while, I start to really hear the breath. As I hear the breath, I come back. I hear the breath, I note the hand on the steering wheel, then I note the emotions and I keep coming back into the thicker and thicker richness of this moment.

There are techniques for coming into the moment through the heart, through energy, through meditation. The beauty of some of the exercises we do—where you focus with another person—is that another person can bring you into the moment. When I do interviews where people focus and look into my eyes, people who aren't used to that start to tell me about their problems. They're looking there or in the papers or something and their eyes flick up every now and then. You're just sitting there. After a while their eyes flicker a few more times and they look at you a little sheepishly, then they quiet down and quiet down until they sort of settle in. Their eyes vibrate and then settle. There's a lot of blinking and then it slows down. It's like a butterfly landing. It's exquisite.

Most people aren't used to looking in each other's eyes except meshugeneh people like us. You don't do it like "You looking at me?" or "Come on, look at me." You don't do it as a power thing. You're just sitting there. When the eyes make contact—not as a social form, not as "Are you here? I'm here, hello in there"—the presence becomes an immense experience of the moment. It becomes very full. Suddenly you are pulled out of your mind, you're pulled out of your plans, you're pulled out of your questions, and you're pulled into the fullness of the moment. When you're around somebody who is in the fullness of the moment, it pulls you in too. That's part of what the richness of a guru is about.

Most of the time we're living in our minds, living in memories, plans, reflections, judgment. The mind is continually presenting thoughts and we're buying them and then identifying with them. We lose the moment when we're off with the thought. We're not there at all. I keep training myself. In my little house, dishes have to be done. When I start to do the dishes, I can feel the difference from when I start to do the dishes to when I end. When I start to do the dishes, I'm busy. I've got to do the dishes so I can get back to my desk or make that phone call. I better do the dishes first. I start out washing the dishes to get done. By the time I'm done, I'm so high from washing the dishes. You can take your moments and train yourself to keep coming back in by just doing what you're doing.

I had an interesting experience at a Benedictine monastery some years back. Life there was very simple and very repetitious, and it was silent. The only time you ever talked was when you were in line to wash your tin plate and you could sort of whisper—a funny little loophole in the system. There was a man in front of me and he had a brush with soap on it and he was washing his tin plate. I was looking over his shoulder and I said, "How long have you been here?" He said, "Seventeen years." The tone of his voice and that brush going around in that plate was so profound, a moment for me of a certain kind of surrender, a certain kind of peacefulness, a certain kind of washing the plate.

The Heart Space

When you are feeling the fullness of the presence of the moment—like this moment with the birds in the background and the movements in the room, my voice and your bodies and the thoughts pouring through your minds—and you get quieter and keep letting the sensations arise and pass away, what is the quality of the heart? It isn't a heavy emotional quality of loving or hating or much intense emotion, but it's a quality of soft presence, of inclusiveness. It's not an emotional space, but it feels to me like a very deep heart space. It's where the quietness of the mind and the heart come together.

Fifteen to twenty years ago, when I first started to meditate Vipassana, I'd end up very dry. Now when I meditate, I end up very moist, very soft, and I realize that I'm appreciating the meditation practice from a different place now. I used to accuse the practice of being dry; now I see it was me who was doing the practice. Now when I do the practice, I end up closer to Maharajji than when I started, even though the practice doesn't believe in gurus and God and all that stuff. I think that as long as you're talking about the heart space as being that quality of boundaryless soft presence and fullness, the quieter your mind and the more you're just here, here, you're appreciating the richness of the moment.

There's nowhere to go because every moment of life, no matter where you are, is equally as rich. It's got so much stuff you haven't examined yet. I was taught a lot by Aldous Huxley, who was a very dear and wonderful writer and philosopher, and we hung out together a little bit. I couldn't really understand most of what he was talking about; he was much too smart for me. The image I have of him all the time was when we were in Copenhagen walking down the street. He was nearly blind but he could see colors and so he was very aware of the colors of light of different countries. He'd talk about Spain as having a certain quality of light. We were walking down the street and a horse had left his calling card on the ground. I said, "Aldous, be careful, there's some horse shit there." Aldous stopped and looked at it. I don't know what he saw, but he said, "E x t r a o r - d i n a r y." And that struck me. Extraordinary. He looked at everything that way.

Those of you who have taken acid . . . There was a moment when I was doing a book on LSD back in the sixties with Sidney Cohen, the "good guy" who worked for the FDA, and I was the "bad guy." We had all these pictures that this photographer had done and Sidney picked all the pictures for the book that made LSD look bad. I picked all the pictures of people making love in fields and playing the flute and things like that. There was one picture both of us picked—a picture of a guy lying on a kitchen floor looking at a puddle from a spilled bottle of Coca-Cola. Sidney picked it as a demonstration of the trivialness of mind when you were in a drugged state. I picked it to show that in everything is everything. In that spilled Coca-Cola was the entire universe in a single moment.

The Changing Moment

Observation will show you that when you arrive at a new situation, the optimum strategy for dealing with that situation is to quiet down and hear the totality of it. You hear all of the variables and how they're all working together in a quiet, intuitive way, out of which will come an optimum action. That is, the more fully you are present in that moment of choice, the more you can expect an optimum response—optimum in the sense of the deepest harmony on most planes of reality. The best practice for being in the moment at *that* moment is to practice being in the moment *this* moment.

Since your planning for that situation is missing the existential components that will exist in that situation but that don't exist now, you are planning in the absence of all the data. For example, I can plan that I'm going to give a lecture next Thursday night, but I don't know whether what I have for dinner that night is going to affect my consciousness in a way that's going to make that lecture other than the one I plan now. What I'm going to do Thursday evening when I'm sitting with that audience is very much a function of what has gone on that day and what I've eaten and what happens in the hall and who comes to the lecture and all that. The minute I make a plan now for what will happen then . . . if I'm so wedded to the plan I had, then I do violence to what the existential moment is in order to impose my plan at that time.

We're all doing that all the time. We're used to having plans and then our inertia of mind, our inability to let go of our plan into the new moment, leaves us strangely out of sync with everything and doing violence to the whole thing. You meet somebody and you have a model of a romance and then you meet them again and the situation offers something entirely different from what you thought it was going to be, but you end up destroying what that new thing could be because you can't hear it because of your attachment to your old model. You begin to observe that phenomenon occurring again and again.

You have to make plans but hold very lightly to them and always realize that the fullness of being in this moment, which includes the future and the plans, is the best preparation for when that time is here now. So being here now is the best preparation for when you are there then, or when there then is here.

The Moment of Death

The moment of death is particularly vivid in Eastern thought, which has reincarnation as an assumption. In those traditions, the moment of death is seen as a significant moment because where your mind is as you leave this incarnation has a lot to do with the vector forces that will determine where you go in the next round. Their understanding is that much of the work you do on yourself in this life is in preparation for being fully present in that moment of death, not with clinging or aversion. They describe a very high monk who had done so much work, and at the moment of his death, a beautiful deer walked past in the distance and he looked at the deer with delight. His mind went out there, and there went a whole birth just for that one thought form.

There's that story of Maharajji where he was sitting on the side of the road near a little temple with some devotees and they ate and they all went to bed around eleven o'clock at night. Around one in the morning, Maharajji got up and started screaming, "I want chapatis and dal [flat bread and lentils], I want chapatis and dal."

They said, "Baba, you already ate."

He said, "I want chapatis and dal."

In India the philosophy is "Who can understand the guru?" So they got up and made the fire and cooked the dal and made the chapatis. It was already two o'clock and Baba ate like he had never seen food before. Then they all went back to bed. The next morning a telegram arrived saying that, down on the plains, about 150 miles away from where he was, one of his old devotees had died at two in the morning. He said, "See? That's why

I wanted the chapatis and dal." They didn't see, but it awakened their curiosity.

After two or three days, like he's talking to children, Baba says, "Don't you understand? As he was dying, he wanted chapatis and dal, and I didn't want him to have to take another birth just for that." So he took it on.

Where you are at the moment of death has to do with what happens next. In view of that, and because of that preoccupation, there is a way of looking at all spiritual practice as preparation for your moment of death. Now, at the moment of death, when the mind, the information system, starts to dissolve . . . in the Tibetan Buddhist system, they say the earth element leaves and you feel heaviness. Then the water element leaves and you feel dryness, thirst. Then the fire element leaves and you feel coldness. Then the air element leaves and the outbreath is longer than the inbreath. I've been around many dying people and it's interesting how when the water element leaves, they'll say, "I'm thirsty." If they're trained properly, they'll say, "Ah, there's thirst, the water element's leaving" versus "I'm thirsty," which will preoccupy them with getting water and start a whole process because everybody is trying to help them. You want water? Here's water. They get all preoccupied with it. If they die at that moment, they'll probably end up as a fish.

I know some of you find this too flip; you think it's serious. Death is the drama that everybody buys into. I treat it rather flip. It's like the Zen master Dahui Zonggao; he's dying and he is supposed to write a death poem. His students are freaked. They say, "You haven't written your death poem yet." He says, "Oh," and he picks up his pen and he does calligraphy madly and he dies. It says, "Birth is thus, death is thus, verse or no verse, what's the fuss?" There's a certain quality of lightness in "Ah, another moment." Death is just another moment, but the minute you are pushing or grabbing, it propels you in a certain direction. You can feel it.

Each moment is a death and birth in which you can feel being propelled by your attractions and aversions. In a way, the whole Eastern strategy is practicing to be here now so that when it really hits the fan, you'll be here now. Dying is like a huge acid trip when it's all dissolving and your mind doesn't work so well and everything's getting kind of weird and it's all changing. This is where change really becomes apparent. To keep equanimity in the presence of change, it's good to practice in advance.

Appreciate the Moment

In the Theravadan Buddhist tradition, the Pali doctrine suggests that because a human birth is so precious and so rare—it's so precious because all the components are necessary for the work of liberation—that you should not waste a moment. You should work as hard as you can and make real effort and not let a moment go by. I do not experience that as true. It's probably true and I'm simply not ready to experience it.

I don't have a sense of urgency about spiritual practice. I have a feeling of the rightness of the unfolding and I have a deep sense of patience about it all. I feel a rhythm in the work and I'll make a really intense effort and then I will pull back and then I'll do other things for a while and play and be in the world. As my spiritual awareness grows, I can feel that the pulling back is as much work as what I thought was the heavy work. It all becomes the same stuff. After a while, there isn't any way to pull back. You can't take a vacation from a spiritual journey.

How can you be kind to yourself, be gentle with yourself? Certainly you should examine things like guilt because you're not working hard enough, all the *oughts* and *shoulds* you drive yourself on ruthlessly with, all those feelings like you're not enough as you are and you ought to be more spiritual and more conscious of something than you are. Appreciate the perfection of the universe, which includes you. You have a right to exist exactly the way you are and you're at the absolutely optimum place at this moment.

If you were fully enlightened, you wouldn't have taken birth here in the first place. This isn't an error. You are not an aberration, you're not an error, you're not somebody's mistake. Nobody blew it. No matter how bizarre you feel from inside, appreciate that it is an unfolding process. You are your curriculum. Baldness was part of my curriculum, having to watch my weight all the time because of this tire around my belly, that's part of my curriculum. Dealing with these issues about retreats, that's my curriculum. There's a certain way of appreciating and allowing and acknowledging *what is* that makes me very gentle with myself.

The Past and the Future

What keeps us from being here now is a combination of the unsatisfactoriness of the present conditions and the karma of the attachments and aversions to past and future. There is attachment to the fantasy of the future rather than to living with what you've got now. You're constantly creating models of how it's all going to come out and who you'll be. It is more comfortable to live as the person who's planning to change, planning to be successful, planning to do all those things than to be fully who you are and facing what you are at this moment.

Rehearsing the past is reassuring to the existence of the separate entity. Most of the thoughts you usually have in some way legitimize an image of yourself that you're trying to preserve. It keeps shoring up the walls of a self-concept, your somebody-ness. It's called "time-binding," where you keep cultivating an image of yourself as an existing entity through constantly rehearsing the past and planning the future. That keeps giving you a support for the image of who you think you are at any moment. So in a way it keeps reassuring you that the prison cell you're in is real when, of course, it is illusory.

There was a stage where I was always time-binding. When I was here with you, I was anticipating the fact that Saturday I'll be at the temple; Sunday I'll be flying to California; Monday I'll be with Creating Our Future; Wednesday I'll be with the teachers; then I'll be in Europe. It was all real at that moment and I constantly had the sequencing of where I came from and where I was going in my mind, so I was always planning and anticipating. I'm a long way away from being cooked, but what's changed now is that much more of the time when I am here, this is it. I'm here. When I'm not here, I'm not here. It's interesting how when you give another human being, your family, or your business the fullness of your being at any moment, a little is enough. When you give them half of it because you're time-binding with your mind, it's never enough.

You can plan for the future. Somebody calls me and says,

"Can I see you next Tuesday at two?" I look in my book and I say, "Yeah." Am I not being in the moment because I'm thinking about the future? The moment is the telephone call, the book, the pencil, the time, the plan in my mind. I'm still here with this whole situation. Next Tuesday the existential situation will be what's in the date book, the telephone ringing, that person's presence, and that'll be that moment.

You could also keep the witness going so that you're aware of your planning. Sometimes when you're planning for something, you lose consciousness so completely that you're not in the present anymore; you are in the future moment. When you are planning for something and somebody comes into the room and you startle, it shows you were so busy in your thought that you lost the moment. Study the way in which your mind works, and you'll see the way in which a concentrated mind deals with the world as opposed to a diffused mind. You see the way in which this lack of integration or this lack of being able to be at the office when you're at the office, and at home when you're at home, reduces your effectiveness in each of them.

The feeling that "I'm not doing enough at home when I'm at work" ends up being you don't do enough at work and you don't do enough at home. If you do your work fully when you're at work and you're home fully when you're at home, by standing back enough in that awareness, you can see the pieces of your life. I have those weekly planners where you stand back and you see what's in your life. I see that I'm working on a book; I see that I have some AIDS patients; I see that I've got Seva; I see that I've got my relationships; I see that I've got the teenage Creating Our Future; I see that I've got the retreats; I see that I've got to rest. I see the pattern of my life and realize "Well, I've overextended myself. I've got too many things, so I'll have to start cutting back till I've got a number that I can handle."

Then I see that each one will take so much time and I stand back and allow those moments when I see the web and the pattern of it all. I'll make a list of all the things I'm involved in, all the different things, and then I'll look and say, "First of all, do they create a life that is fulfilling my unique opportunities in the universe? Am I understanding each of them as part of my spiritual path because that's what my business is about? Is each one appropriate? Do I want to phase it out or do I want to keep it? Should it take a bigger part of my life?" I stand back and I get a feeling of the design of my life. Once I'm at peace with the design of my life, then when I'm at each thing, the other part of me that has already stood back and seen the design of it is at peace and I can fully be in the thing I'm in. It's when it's undigested and you don't stand back and get that perspective that you are constantly feeling you're not doing *this* when you're doing *that*.

I'm giving you a little plan of action. One is cultivating the spacious awareness that sees the whole thing before you, and the other is the practice of "When I'm here, I'm here." The best gift you can bring to everything that's going to come up in your life in the future is to do what you're doing at this moment fully.

Trapped in Old Models

I was already old in the sixties, but I was an uncle of the sixties, and in the sixties we all had the feeling of living in "be here now," living in the moment and changing as fast as you wanted to change. Run it up the flagpole and see who salutes.

Let's do the right thing at this moment. Ideas like sustainability or persistence or patience or continuity were the establishment words. They weren't the words of the New Age, where you're with a person as long as it feels good and if it doesn't, screw it. It changed a lot of social patterns.

When I became involved in Seva, I was still that person and it was very exciting to start a program helping to eradicate blindness in Nepal. After five years, there was still a lot of blindness in Nepal. I thought, My God, I'm sucked into this game. I can't get out. I kept saying to everybody, "I think I'll quit. I think I've had enough." Then I had to face the fact that this was an opportunity for me to learn other qualities of life. Freedom wasn't external freedom; it was internal freedom and I was confusing my freedom to shift games with freedom. I was trapped with a model about what rush I needed from life that made me want to shift all the time.

I spent years saying I'd rather be in Bali, so I'd go to Bali and then I'd be as neurotic in Bali as I was in Boston. I'd think, Well, what I really need is to be in southern Italy, so I'd go to southern Italy. Well, what I need is really a love affair. And I'd go do that. I kept running from here to there.

I was in Japan in a Zendo and we used to chant the seventeenth-century poem "Hakuin's Song of Zazen" every morning aloud. One of the lines is "Your coming-and-going takes place nowhere else but where you are." There I was in Japan on my way from India back to the States. "Your coming-and-going takes place nowhere else but where you are." And I started to sense that there's a place in me where there's no coming-and-going. I get on the plane and the plane flies its heart out and then I end up here and I'm still here. Where did

I go? And that was the meaning of "be here now." Where could you go anyway?

Once I started to realize that, then going everywhere and collecting more experiences started to lose its power over me. You begin to see that you don't have to keep collecting experiences; it's all inside you. It's enough. You can be with enough. Working out of enough-ness instead of the need for more is a great art form, and an entrance into be here now.

REFLECTION ON COMPASSION AND EQUANIMITY

by Joseph Goldstein

Joseph Goldstein has been leading insight and loving-kindness meditation retreats worldwide since 1974. He is a cofounder of the Insight Meditation Society in Barre, Massachusetts, where he is on the guiding teachers' Founders Council. In 1989, he helped establish the Barre Center for Buddhist Studies.

Joseph became interested in Buddhism when he was a Peace Corps volunteer in Thailand in 1965. He has studied under eminent teachers from India, Burma, and Tibet and is the author of Mindfulness: A Practical Guide to Awakening*;* A Heart Full of Peace*;* One Dharma: The Emerging Western Buddhism*;* Insight Meditation: The Practice of Freedom*;* The Experience of Insight: A Simple and Direct Guide to Buddhist Meditation*; and coauthor with Jack Kornfield of* Seeking the Heart of Wisdom: The Path of Insight Meditation.

Here, Joseph talks about two qualities of mind that provide an avenue into deeper self-awareness.

How can we stay open and responsive to the many challenges in our lives, both individually and collectively in our society, without becoming overwhelmed or drowning in the difficulties that arise?

As we start paying attention to the situations we face, two qualities of mind emerge as being particularly effective—the qualities of *equanimity* and *compassion*. We usually hear more about compassion because most spiritual traditions value its cultivation. Equanimity is a more subtle and perhaps invisible quality of mind, one that may be more difficult to recognize and cultivate. Yet equanimity and compassion are very intimately connected.

What is equanimity? It's the mind space of impartiality—a nonreactive easefulness of mind that is open to seeing the whole of different situations and experiences.

The poet Rainer Maria Rilke wrote some beautiful lines about the possibility of seeing things as a whole. He was talking about interpersonal relationships, but it really applies to all of our experience. He wrote, "Once the realization is accepted that even between the closest human beings infinite distances continue to exist, a wonderful living side by side can grow up, if they succeed in loving the distance between them, which makes it possible for each to see the other whole and against a wide sky." I find the image of an immense sky so beautiful. We might say that equanimity is like that expanse, the space that holds everything, that holds all the world. It gives us the opportunity to see each other and all situations as a whole before an immense sky, before the immense space of our minds.

This spaciousness does not imply a lack of discernment or a state of vague confusion. Equanimity is a state of mind that is open and clear. In its nonreactivity, it helps us see things without bias. When we're caught up in reactions to things, we're not seeing things as a whole; we're seeing things through the lens of partiality. Equanimity allows us to see the whole of another person, the whole of a situation. It's the basis then for wise discernment and skillful responsiveness.

The question then is, How do we cultivate equanimity, both in our meditation practice and in our daily lives with all their busyness and challenges? You undoubtedly have seen how quickly our minds can become reactive, whether to pleasant or unpleasant things. One way of exploring this is through reframing our experience. In difficult situations, whether it's with one person or a larger situation in our lives, there are a couple of questions we might use to extricate ourselves from the quagmire of our conditioned and habitual reactions.

For example, quite a few years ago, I was at an IMS board meeting, and it was particularly contentious. Now I even forget what the issue was, but I do remember the contention. People were really attached to their views, and I was really attached to my view, which, of course, I felt to be the correct one! I was feeling the tension in the room and the tension and suffering in myself, which prompted an interest to investigate: "What's going on here?" Then I asked myself a very simple question: "Why do the other people feel the way they do?" When I asked that question, I realized there must be a reason why others were holding their views. My mind expanded a bit and I began to see things from their viewpoint, which greatly eased that sense of polarity, of conflict.

Then the following question came to me: "What can I learn from this situation?" A very simple reframing had turned a difficult experience into a vehicle for opening my mind, for becoming more equanimous, for understanding other points of view.

This reframe is not difficult to do; it's simply difficult to remember to do in the heat of our attachment to our own views. Sometimes, when we find ourselves reactive, this investigation of our own minds can become an invitation for us to look inward rather than to stay in the mode of blaming or judging others. Liberation always comes from examining our own minds.

Another reflection that helps support greater equanimity is realizing that much of what happens in our lives is outside of our control, even though it's often hard to believe that we are not actually the governing center of the universe. When things are beyond our range of influence, can we rest in equanimity? And somewhat paradoxically, the more we let go of the illusion of being in control, the more clearly we can see what causes and conditions can give rise to that which fulfills our aims. We might say that in these situations, it empowers us to work from the bottom up rather than from the top down.

Equanimity also grows from an increasing awareness of *impermanence*. We all know intellectually that things change. It is not an esoteric truth. However, even though we know the truth of impermanence conceptually, we are not living our lives in accordance with this truth. If we were, we would not cling to that which in its very nature is always becoming otherwise. This rapid flow of change is always taking place, and seeing this impermanence, this change, helps us be less reactive to what's happening. We don't have to be so disturbed by difficulties if we realize it's all part of the passing show.

As we develop and practice equanimity in our lives, we also need to be aware of a hidden danger—what the Buddha called the "near enemies" of wholesome states. Compassion and equanimity each has a corresponding quality of mind that looks like it but is not it. The near enemy of equanimity is *indifference*, a withdrawal from experience. When you're indifferent, you don't care about other people. It's a nonresponsiveness to life, which is very different from equanimity—that open, clear awareness of all aspects of our experience. In this clear seeing, we are better able to discern where we can be effective, what wholesome states should be cultivated, what unwholesome states should be let go of and abandoned. We begin to see that when there's equanimity rather than indifference, we can engage with all of life in a meaningful way.

Equanimity is also the foundation for compassion to arise. Compassion arises out of the willingness to come close to suffering, and, with equanimity, we have enough stability and openness of mind to see the whole of a situation. It provides the strength and stability to come close to the suffering that may exist without reactivity. But this is sometimes a challenge because we often don't want to come close to suffering, to pain either in ourselves or in others. Our tendency is to avoid it. But when our hearts and minds are open to difficulties, and we are willing to come close to suffering, what happens is that quite naturally we develop a greater empathy for the person, for the situation, or for ourselves because we're willing to stand in the presence of it. Out of this empathy, a compassion-inducing question arises: "How can I help?" This is the title of a book by Ram Dass and Paul Gorman and it so captures the essence of compassion.

Empathy is feeling what somebody else is going through, feeling and attuning to the suffering that may be there. Compassion implies an action; it implies a responsiveness. We might sometimes think that compassion only manifests as some heart-opening feeling that is splendid and vast. But compassion may express itself in more ordinary ways. I like to think of compassion as responsiveness: if somebody's hungry, you feed them. It's just the natural response of an open heart, and that openheartedness to suffering is more possible when there's equanimity.

But just as equanimity can slide into indifference, compassion has its own near enemy, which is *sorrow*. While the feeling of sadness can open the heart to the suffering that's there, overwhelming sorrow simply leads to despair about the situation, which makes it difficult to act. Sorrow masquerades as compassion, and it hinders the very essence of compassion, so well expressed by Thich Nhat Hanh: "Compassion is a verb."

As we learn to navigate the challenges of our lives and the suffering that we inevitably encounter, it's helpful to deepen our exploration of the meaning and experience of equanimity and compassion. The potential for equanimity and compassion and wisdom exists in all of us, and they can become the guiding polestar of our lives.

THE PRACTICE OF MEDITATION

by Ram Dass

Meditation is one of the most basic practices on the spiritual path, but one size does not fit all. There are different types of meditation practices, and you may wind up doing various types at different times along the way.

Mindfulness meditation focuses on nonjudgmental awareness of the moment. Vipassana, also called "insight meditation," is an ancient practice that combines mindfulness and scanning the body with insight into the nature of reality, and can also be done as a walking meditation. Another Buddhist technique is lovingkindness (metta) meditation, which deepens feelings of love and kindness toward others and oneself. Mantra meditation involves concentration on the repetition of a seed syllable (like om *or* ram*) or a phrase; TM (Transcendental Meditation) is a well-known mantra meditation practice. Chakra meditation concentrates on the body's seven main energy centers to keep them open and aligned. You could also meditate on the guru, a particular deity, or any aspect of the divine with which you resonate.*

In a group setting, a teacher will often offer a guided meditation, which takes the group into a certain bhav*—the spiritual feelings and absorption into the presence of God or the guru or love and wisdom.*

Here Ram Dass takes us on guided meditation journeys into awareness, the breath, and oneness with it all. Consider recording these meditations and listening back to them when you sit.

Awareness Meditation

Sit quietly and be aware. Be aware of the sound. Be aware of the sun and the feeling of the warmth on your head and your skin. Be aware of the feelings in your body, of the children's voices. The clear smell of the air. Be aware of this moment in history. Be aware of this in context that it's this day, this month, this year, and everything each one of those things implies.

Sitting here in your awareness, be aware of the earth upon which you sit and its age relative to our history. Know that the ocean and the land reach back to "in the beginning." See that we are here among the generations. There are children, there are parents, and there are parents' parents. Or looked at another way, there are people, there are their children, and there are their children's children.

Be aware of your stage or point of incarnation. So many years passed, an unknown number yet to come. But see that in each moment, in this moment, is all of it.

This moment contains all of us—those of us who are caught in hatred and violence, in fear, in loneliness, in hunger, in being the objects of prejudice. It's all here right now.

For us to live in the moment means to have a quiet mind and an open heart, to honor the preciousness of a human birth, to treat our bodies as temples and to take proper care of them without clinging to them when it is time to discard them like worn-out garments.

Be aware as you sit here of the senses in your body, the sun, the bird, the child. Be aware of it all.

Breath Meditation

Sit quietly and feel your way into this moment—sounds, sensations of the seat or the floor under your body, feeling the air on your skin, all the thoughts that are coming and going. Experience it all as if you're on the bank of a river, watching the leaves float by on the water.

Thoughts come and go and sensations come and go. Be mindful of each thing as it arises, not holding it or pushing it away. Pains, confusion, fear, planning, memories, tension in the body, sensations and sounds, smell, taste—be with each thing just as it is. Not pushing, not pulling.

Become aware of the breath. The breath is one of the things that just is. Be aware of the inbreath and the outbreath. Then imagine you have nostrils in the middle of your chest so the breath is going in and out of the chest. Imagine that as you draw the breath in through the chest, what you're drawing in along with the air is an elixir, a soma, a moist, very sweet, soft light, a quality of light or sound. You draw it in and it fills your being. It goes up into your head, into your arms, to your legs and torso. It fills your being.

And as you let the breath out, the healing stuff that pours through your body is able to dislodge fear, tension, resistance. Let it go and then once again draw in light. The outbreath is almost like a sigh. You realize that what's going out of your body is not what is. It's the resistance against what is.

After you've done a few of those breaths and you've let go of what you can, turn it a little bit so that you're breathing in that healing light and you're breathing that same healing light out into the universe. You are almost like a beacon, a conduit through which energy is passing and coming forth out of the heart. The outbreath as light, as love, as presence, as is-ness. C. S. Lewis said, "There seems no centre because it is all centre." Your heart is the center of the entire universe. Imagine concentric circles around you, spreading as far as the mind can imagine. All human beings, all beings of all species, all beings of the past, all beings of the future, beings on other planes as well as on this one, as far as the mind can imagine, all these beings in every direction around you.

Now, from the middle of your heart, send out on the outbreath to those beings, to all beings everywhere, the blessing of your light.

Shanti. Shanti. Shanti.

Oneness Meditation

Imagine a tiny being, the size of your thumb, sitting on a lotus flower right in the middle of your chest. As you look upon this being, light is pouring forth from it. It is radiant, luminous, and just from looking upon this being, you get a sense of incredible peace. You look at its face and you feel infinite compassion within this being. Just being near this entity fills you with a feeling of love. It sits quietly, with perfect equanimity and great wisdom.

Now let that being grow in size till it fills your body. Its head, your head. Its torso, your torso. Its legs, your legs. Its arms, your arms. Feel its peace, feel its equanimity. Let yourself be filled with its love.

Now, with your eyes closed, you and the being expand in size until your head reaches to the ceiling and all of us are within you and this voice is within you. Feel your hugeness. Now you break out of the building, your head going up into the sky. Your head is among the planets. You have grown in size till you are sitting in the middle of this galaxy, this universe. The earth is within your belly. Feel your hugeness at this moment. You are in the silence of the heavens. Expand yet again until all of the planets, all of the galaxies, everything of which you can think is within you.

You are the One. You are the Ancient One. I am within you. Everything that ever was, is, or will be is part of the dance of your being. You are all of the universe, so you have infinite wisdom. You appreciate all of the feelings of the universe, so you have infinite compassion. Feel your immensity, your aloneness.

Now let the boundaries of your being disintegrate, and merge yourself into that which is beyond form. Sit for a moment in the formless. There is nothing but the One.

Gently reestablish the form of your being and very slowly reduce in size back through the universe. Smaller, smaller, until your head is at the roof of this building. Look down and find who you thought you were. Look at that being. Look at her or his life. Look at that being as a soul, living out another round. Look upon that being with compassion. See how it gets lost into its drama at this moment. Reach down from your vast height and gently touch that being in blessing on the top of its head. At this moment, you are that which blesses and you are that which is being blessed.

Now come down in size until you are back into your body, still with this radiant being filling you, this being of peace, love, passion, wisdom, this being who in its huge form fills the universe and who now fills your body. As this being, hold your right palm forward and allow yourself to become a vehicle for bringing those qualities out into the physical plane to all beings who suffer in the universe. Become a pure vehicle of that huge one. Let it pour through your hand. Feel it coming out of the palm of your right hand, and send blessings of peace and love to all beings who suffer, whether their suffering is physical, psychological, or spiritual.

If there are beings who are suffering, bring them to mind and surround their beings with light, with love, and with peace. At this moment, if there are beings toward whom you feel anger, bring them into your consciousness. See the soul that lies within that incarnation and bless that soul with love and peace and light. For as you go on this spiritual journey, you must accept the responsibility to share what you receive, for that is part of the harmony of God. You become an instrument for the manifestation of the will of God.

Now put your hand down and finally let that being become smaller and smaller until it is the size of a thumb once more, sitting in the middle of your heart. That is your inner guru. That is the inner voice that speaks truth because it is truth. That is the being who will guide you home. That is the being that is none other than your true self when you finish being who you think you are.

At any time, you can go inside and talk to and listen to that being, whether you call it Christ or Buddha or God or guru or your true self.

PART III

Coming into Wholeness

Self is everywhere, shining forth from all beings,
vaster than the vast, subtler than the most subtle,
unreachable, yet nearer than breath, than heartbeat.
Eye cannot see it, ear cannot hear it nor tongue
utter it; only in deep absorption can the mind,
grown pure and silent, merge with the formless truth.
He who finds it is free; he has found himself;
he has solved the great riddle; his heart forever
  is at peace.
Whole, he enters the Whole.
His personal self returns to its radiant, intimate,
  deathless source.

—*Mundaka Upanishad*

Chapter 9

The Teachers—Everyone and Everything

How are we going to get to wholeness? Our paths may seem hidden, or they may fork in different directions, and we may struggle with obstacles as we cling to our beliefs as to how the path should proceed. Who will lead us, direct us, teach us what we need to know?

As we learned in India when we were there with Ram Dass and Maharajji, there is a big difference between a teacher, called an "upaguru," and the enlightened satguru. An upaguru is a teacher who can show you the way, the next steps along your path. It literally means "the teacher nearby," so basically anyone or anything can be a teacher. For example, you might have a golf guru or a diet guru, an expert who can point you in the right direction for that particular goal. You could also receive teachings from the tree outside your window or the cat curled in your lap.

The satguru is another story. "Sat" means truth in Sanskrit, and "guru" translates to "the remover of darkness," so the satguru is the "true guru," the fully liberated rishi, or saint, whose whole purpose is to guide you to the realization of the self through the realization of God, the one who takes you from the darkness of ignorance to the light of awakened consciousness. Neem Karoli Baba, Ram Dass's Maharajji, is such a being, recognized as a saint throughout India, who is still "with" us even though he left his body in 1973.

In this chapter, Ram Dass talks about teachers, the upagurus who guide us a certain way along our paths. Ram Dass said the upaguru was the teacher standing next to you by the road, while the satguru beckoned from up the road at the destination. And he reminds us that the guru doesn't necessarily have to be in form.

As Ram Dass says in Polishing the Mirror, *"If you see everything in the universe as a way to work on your own consciousness—even if it's showing you where you're unconscious or where you're asleep—then everyone and everything in the universe becomes your teacher and is a means of awakening."*

I spoke to Timothy [Leary] last week. He called me from San Diego, where he is still in prison; he expects to be out very shortly. He's writing and seems in good spirits and doesn't seem to have changed a bit. I love Timothy a great deal as a person, but I don't feel I have any work to do with him. He was a great teacher for me in the early sixties. The way it is with teachers, you take a teaching, and sometimes that teaching will take you all the way, and sometimes you must leave that teacher and go on, no blame. You don't have to judge a teacher and say that teacher isn't good enough. You just have to say that I don't have any work to do with that teacher at this moment. That's enough. You don't have to analyze everybody's clay feet. You will know in your heart.

You will notice in your own development that you will get fed in a certain way, and then you will yearn for, say, a quieting of your mind. You'll start to look around for meditation space and people who can help you with meditation. You'll start to see how your body freaked out and your whole consciousness was captured by the pain in your knees, so you figure you've got to get your body together and that will lead you into some kind of physical training, and you will listen for that kind of a teacher.

At first, the spiritual journey is very eclectic. You take a little of this and a little of that. You quiet the mind, you open the heart, you sing with one group and you meditate with another, and so on. That's all fine. As you get further along the path, you begin to feel a pull toward one ray or a particular lineage. It's not a lineage necessarily determined by your strong points. It might even be by your weak points. It might be a lineage of the heart and you've been in your head; you'll feel pulled in that direction and you won't like it. You'll hate everybody involved, but you can't stop because you know its rightness for you.

The secret is listening to the truth that's coming from your inner being. If in doubt, sit down and go inside and ask. If you ask in purity and can quiet your mind, you'll hear some kind of an answer. At least usually.

I had a very interesting dialogue with Chögyam Trungpa Rinpoche, who's a tantric rascal. Many years ago I went to hear one of his lectures in Vermont. I was waiting out in the parking lot, hanging out with some friends, smoking a joint, getting ready to go hear his lecture. A messenger came and told me that Trungpa wanted to see me. I'd only heard one of his lectures and I'd never met him before. I was brought into this room and he was sitting there in a chair with his bottle of sake next to him. There was only one chair, so I knelt on the floor in front of him. He looked at me and said, "Ram Dass, we have to accept responsibility."

I didn't quite know what to do with that, so I countered with a bhakti retort. I said, "What responsibility? God has all the responsibility. Not my but thy will, O Lord." I felt very good.

He said, "You're copping out." And that was the end of our discussion.

That was the teaching at that moment. And I hung with that for years and years and years, trying to figure out what the hell he was talking about.

In this journey, there is nothing wrong with not knowing, or with falling on your face. If you make mistakes and fall on your face, you get up, brush yourself off, and get on with it. You say, "Ah, this is my teacher. You are so pure. I love you. I want to study with you," and then you learn the teacher is sleeping with your friend or asking for large sums of money. Well, I blew it. It wasn't the pure teacher I expected. Okay, thank you for your teaching. On you go.

Just keep taking the teachings. Take the teachings. When the time comes, you'll feel a pull into wanting to go deeper and deeper in your surrender and your trust and you'll find a teacher who will take you much deeper. You are tuned in such a way that your perception is open to finding the beings you need.

God has a great sense of humor. Don't get caught in models as to what a teacher is going to look like, because they never look like they're supposed to, believe me. I took teachings from a Brooklyn housewife. You can't figure out the models at all. You may end up going on a journey of thousands and thousands of miles and then coming back to Oklahoma City to find out that it was your Aunt Doris, who all the time was the Buddha in drag, stirring the chicken soup, waiting for you to get back so she could feed you.

Physical Plane Teachers

It is very useful to have teachers on the physical plane when the opportunity presents itself. If the opportunity doesn't present itself, don't feel that you are blowing the scene. That isn't true at all. You can still use every experience in your life to become closer to God. But when you find a teacher whom you can trust, then it is useful because that teacher will help you clean up your ego in ways that you would be inclined to slide over.

It is useful because the teacher will show you, through their mirroring and their training, where you're holding your secret stash of attachment. They will help you uncover your attachments just by shining the light of clarity and truth. The problem is there are very few teachers that are totally pure. Very often a teacher has a set of subtle attachments, and the student gets into a relationship where the teacher's attachments keep the student from seeing herself or himself clearly enough. When you get involved with a teacher, keep listening with your heart, not your emotional heart but with your inner voice. Even if everybody around you tells you it's right on, this is the way you should be going, if it doesn't feel right to you, trust that.

But even if they themselves may not be the full truth, a teacher can be someone through whom a teaching comes. Think of all teachers as teachings, then you don't have to sit around judging them. Is this one good enough to be my guru? It's a drag to think about it. It'll just get you into a cop-out of saying, "I don't have a guru." Looking for the guru is as much coming to God as finding the guru, so you can spend your life looking for gurus and that'll get you there too. It's like making pilgrimages to holy places. It's not the getting there; it's the going that gets you there.

Fierce Teachers

There's a great story about a samurai who comes to a monk for teachings and says, "Monk, teach me about heaven and hell."

The monk looks up at this huge warrior and says, "Teach you about heaven and hell? You call yourself a samurai? You're dirty, you smell, your sword looks rusty. Who would hire you as a samurai? You're a fool. You look stupid. I couldn't teach you about heaven and hell."

The veins on the neck of the samurai stand out. His face gets all red. Finally, he loses it completely and whips out his sword to kill this insolent monk. And the monk says, "That's hell."

The samurai immediately sheaths his sword, realizing what teaching he's been given—that the monk has just offered his life, literally, for this teaching—and he bows in honor. The monk says, "And that is heaven."

I love stories about fierce teachings, like this one about a guru up in the mountains in the Kumaon Hills. His name was Sombari Maharaj and he was a very, very far-out man with great powers, an enlightened and compassionate being. He had an old devotee who was very devoted to him. One day he said to the devotee, "Here, take these two potatoes and go down by the river and eat them." So the devotee took the two potatoes and went down to the river and started to eat the first potato.

He was halfway through the potato when a beggar came along and said, "You already have one potato and I'm very hungry. Would you give me the other potato?" This man is a good man. What could he do? He already had one potato, so of course he gave the other potato to the beggar.

When he finished eating the potato, he went back to Sombari Maharaj. As he climbed the hill and came into sight, Sombari Maharaj is screaming at him, "You fool, you bloody fool. You gave away the second potato. I guess it's not in your destiny to have eaten a second potato. Ah, well, such is karma."

This man became very successful in the world. His children all grew up healthy, married, and became successful. He had many grandchildren. That was the first potato. That's the end of the story, and that's about as heavy as stories get. Of course, it turned out that the beggar was no other than Sombari Maharaj.

What we're talking about here is eating the second potato. It's the moment when you are willing to give up even your values of what's good—feeding a hungry beggar—in order to be free, which requires a faith that when you are free, you will be and do good. Isn't that far-out?

No Better Teacher than Family

There's usually no better teacher than your family. At the time of my parents' fortieth wedding anniversary, my mother was very ill, close to death. My brothers and I had prepared a big, beautiful photographic album of their whole life together, with pictures and poems, and it was art. It had taken me months of sneaking into their house at night to sneak negatives out and to do all this stuff. I was to present it at a brunch we were having at my brother's house. It was New Year's Day, January 1, which was their anniversary.

Well, I was at Harvard at that time, and the night before we had a major psychedelic session in our living room. I had timed it wrong, so that in the morning, when I looked in the mirror to shave to go to the brunch, there was no face. I thought, Now don't get scared. Don't freak. You're under this chemical and you're not seeing your face. Just close your eyes and shave. I do live a little on the edge. I started to drive to the gathering and the steering wheel kept turning into a snake and I looked at the people in the street and they were all speaking a foreign language. I didn't even know what country I was in. Then I thought, Look, you're scaring yourself. Turn it off. Just go to your brother's.

I walked into my brother's house and what I saw was that all my relatives were in their more simian form. They all looked like monkeys. My grandmother was up in a tree scratching herself. All the family looked like each other, these big and little monkeys. I was wearing dark sunglasses since my pupils were like headlights. The night before had been New Year's Eve, so everybody assumed that I had been drunk. I didn't tell them I was stoned.

So I'm talking to these chimps and it's all very friendly. We sit down to brunch. Now, my family has an old and noble tradition in which you express love by cutting each other to ribbons, something that you may not be familiar with in your family, but I know it well. My brother was sitting across the table and I saw his mouth open and he said, "Well, how's the nut business?" I was a therapist at Harvard, a professor of psychology. How's the nut business? I saw his mouth open and an arrow come out of his mouth. With my psychic hand I reached up and took the arrow and put it down next to my spoon.

Then I looked at him and I said, "Gee, your children have grown up so beautifully. They are good-looking and healthy and wonderful." I felt this heart come out of my mouth and slowly go across the table and hit him in the head. He had a look of confusion because I wasn't playing by the rules, you see? It hit him, but it confused him.

The next thing he said was "Well, you haven't grown any more hair, have you?" I saw that arrow come across and I put it down next to the first arrow. I said, "Your wife, Helen, is so beautiful. And it's such fun to see that you've been so caring as a parent." A heart went across the table. Again, a look of confusion.

That afternoon, we were all sitting in the living room, all of us in chairs huddled together, parents with kids in their arms. Nobody could figure out what was going on. I mean, this wasn't our family. Everybody was totally in love with everybody else. We got out on the street and nobody wanted to get in their car and go away. So I figured: I'm seeing this because I'm drugged. They're probably fighting like usual and I'm not seeing it. I'm a scientist too, so I figured I'd wait for independent data. The next day they called up and said, "Wasn't that an incredible day!"

If somebody like my brother comes along and can get to me, gets me uptight or awakens some desire in me, wow, I am delighted they got me! That's my work on myself. If I'm angry with you because your behavior doesn't fit my model of how you should be, that's my problem for having models. No expectations, no upset. It's interesting to move to the level where you can appreciate love instead of constantly bringing in that judging component, which is really rooted in your own feelings of lack of power. Judging comes out of your own fear. I fall prey to it all the time, but every time I do, I catch myself.

If you've got the game working right, every situation that comes up in your life is a vehicle for you to come into a deeper attunement with the deepest part of your being, with Christ consciousness, with the universe, with the laws of the cosmos, et cetera. Everything. When somebody attacks you, when somebody doesn't attack you, when somebody surrenders in a business dealing—all of it works the same way. You're taking the juice from the universe and you're moving it all in a way to become more centered, more quiet.

Teaching Methods

All methods are traps. I, as a teacher, am a trap. Bhakti is a trap. Gurus are traps. The whole shtick is a trap. The concept of God is a trap. But you don't try to cross the ocean of existence without a boat unless you can fly; if you can't fly, you use the boat. When you get to the far shore, you don't stick the boat on your shoulder and keep carrying it. You leave it there. You can't ride in a boat and be so afraid of being in the boat that you've got one foot out.

You see, the thing about a method is that for a method to work, it has to trap you. If you try to dilettante your way through, it doesn't work. You've got to become a meditator. But if you end up a meditator, you lost; you want to end up free, not a meditator. There are a lot of people who just end up meditators. It's the golden chain of righteousness that caught them again. A method must trap you, and then, finally, if it works, it self-destructs and you come through the other end and you're free of method. That's the story.

That's what *The Gospel of Sri Ramakrishna* is so wonderful about; Ramakrishna went through Kali worship and then came out and started to explore all the other methods. Once you come through your method, all methods lead you to the same thing. People say to me, "You do Buddhist meditation and you've got a Hindu guru and you're a Jew?" I say, "I don't have any problem with that. What's your problem? It seems fine for me."

You can't follow practices out of *oughts* and *shoulds*, out of guilt and shame and unworthiness. They aren't worth a damn if you do it that way. If you are doing your sadhana because you think you ought to be good or you ought to get holy, forget it. Go out and have a hamburger, go to a porno flick, and start all over again. Because phony holies don't get there. You may be busy making believe none of this exists. Making believe this never happened. Go ahead, I dare you. You can't get away with that because you're hooked. Just try to get out of this now. Go back and live life just like everybody else? Forget it. You can make believe you're just going to live life, to hell with all this, but it'll sneak in on you. There's no way out. Once you have awakened, you can't get back to sleep. I'm sorry to report it's just a cleanup operation from here on out for the next thousand lifetimes or so.

Eastern Teachers in the West

Starting in the sixties, there was an influx of Eastern spiritual teachers to the West. I remember going to the Avalon Ballroom in the company of Sufi Sam to hear Allen Ginsberg introduce A. C. Bhaktivedanta, who was going to chant this weird chant called "Hare Krishna." And that was just in the early sixties. The Beatles, of course, were jetting around with Maharishi Mahesh Yogi.

The predicament was that many of the Eastern teachers who came over to the West had come out of primarily celibate renunciate paths. They weren't ready for Western women, who were in the middle of their sexual freedom and feminism. So these men teachers were absolutely vulnerable and fell like flies. These people were teachers, upagurus, not satgurus. A true guru is a cooked goose; a true guru is done. The difference between a cave and a city makes no difference to a true guru. To a teacher it makes a hell of a lot of difference because a teacher is pointing the way, while a guru *is* the way, and it's a very different quality.

We bring our judging mind to bear on a whole scene. I was surrounded by people coming up to me with gossip about what this spiritual teacher or that spiritual teacher had done. It seemed like everybody was becoming a connoisseur of clay feet. They were busy deciding whether they could afford to take teachings from somebody who was impure. They were looking for the impurities in order to protect themselves because they misunderstood the concept of surrender. They thought you surrendered to somebody else as a person, when what you really surrender to is the truth.

Surrender

Surrender is tricky. "Surrender" is a very unpleasant word to us in the West. The fact that surrender is such a deep part of the spiritual path is something that we have had to stretch a great deal to understand. We tend to have a very hard time surrendering to other beings that are in physical bodies. We sit around judging them rather than surrendering to them.

Most people we call gurus are really teachers whose goose is not fully cooked. Most of them are still working out their own stuff. But if you surrender to another being in purity, even if they're impure, your purity will free you, even as their impurity will entrap them. You don't have to spend too much time worrying about the purity of your teachers. Take what teachings are around, take them with a pure heart, with a true desire for God, and you'll get what you need.

Your intuitive heart has to be the final arbiter of where the truth lies. You are surrendering to God in the form of another person. They are merely a vehicle through which, if there is a purity in your heart in the way you seek truth, you separate the purity of their message from the stuff of their karma, as the swan is able to separate milk from water. In Hindu mythology, the swan, the Hamsa, represents the soul's discernment, its ability to distinguish between what is real and what is illusion. The soul can extract what is pure from what is sullied, as the mythic swan can extract pure milk from dirty water. You take whatever resonates with you as truth from a teacher, even an impure teacher, and you work with it.

Some teachers will say, "I've given you so much, you've got to do this for me." I would say the only thing you owe a teacher is for you to get enlightened.

You've got to hear that surrender is no surrender at all because the highest thing in the other person is the same as the highest thing in you. The fact is that you can't really decide to surrender because that's just another power trip—I'm surrendering to you; give me the truth. It doesn't work that way. The relationship between a pure master and a *chela* [student, disciple] has nothing to do with the intellect whatsoever. There's no choice involved at all. It's a deep karmic unfolding when the moment is right.

Mahatma Gandhi, one of my great teachers, says, "God demands nothing less than complete self-surrender." It's the price for the only freedom that is worth having. When someone loses themselves, they immediately find themselves in the service of all that lives. It becomes their delight and recreation. They're never wary of spending themselves in the service of God's creation.

It reminds me of the story of the pig and chicken walking down the street. They're hungry and they want breakfast and they come to a restaurant. They start to go in and the pig says, "I'm not going in there."

"Why not?"

"Because there's a sign that says 'ham and eggs.'"

The chicken says, "Oh, come on, we'll have something else."

The pig says, "Look, it's fine for you. All they want from you is a contribution; from me they want total surrender."

The Wrong Teacher

You may choose the wrong teacher. You may get into a method that's not good for you. Many things may happen. This trip is based on total honesty with yourself, total honesty. If you make a mistake, admit it and get on with it. Don't cover your errors. If you were perfect, you wouldn't need to go on a journey. And don't be afraid of making errors. An error can be corrected, as long as you can do so without hurting another being. These are spiritual opportunities. Another rule of this game is you may never use one soul for another. If your journey to God is keeping another being from going to God, forget it. You're never going to get there. It's as simple as that. Listen to yourself and be honest with yourself. Listen inward and be honest.

Now, when you listen inward, you may not even know what to listen to. There are dozens of voices saying, "Listen to me. I'm the one. See? I'm the one. Get all you can. I'm the one. Give it all up." It's the superego in your ear. All of these voices are vying to be center stage, while you keep listening for what the Quakers call the "still, small voice" within you. Listen deeper and quieter and deeper and quieter. The more you enter a meditative space, the clearer you'll hear your dharma, your flow, your route back to the Source, your way home.

What you saw in that teacher was living spirit, so you don't want to recover from that. What you want to recover from is confusing that living spirit by identifying with a form. Forms come and forms go. My guru dropped his body in 1973. What I had with him, I still have with him although the form isn't there anymore. I miss the form, but that's just missing the form. It didn't destroy the essence between us.

If the teacher is impure, that's his karma, not mine. What you buy of it is yours. When you've invested years believing in a certain teacher and then your belief in them isn't strong enough anymore, there is grief. You work with it, allowing yourself to have a grief reaction. You can't rush grief reactions. Sometimes they take several years. I worked with a woman named Joya for a long time. When I left Joya, it took me almost two years before my heart fully opened again because it hurt so bad. I felt I had no more work to do with her, but still my heart hurt.

Learning how to say no to people with love, or leaving a teacher with love, has to do with not closing your heart to another human being, even though they may be threatening you or hurting you. It's like Christ saying of the soldiers, "Forgive them, Lord. They know not what they do." It's that same place. At the same moment, Christ says, "I come with a sword." And he does turn the tables over in the temple. He does do assertive things.

I was dealing with a publisher on the contract for one of my books. When I first met him, I could feel him seeing me as a spiritual space case who he was going to be able to manipulate from a business point of view. I quieted down and said, “Look, I really feel a great warmth toward you and I feel that you and I are to be dear friends, but now we are in contract negotiations and I’m not going to let you screw me to the wall.” For me not to be impeccable, to let him hurt me or let him exploit me, I have the karma on me. So sometimes you are defending yourself. That’s what aikido is about, that your actions toward your opponent are a compassionate act to help that being bring the energies into harmony.

Judging Teachers

We may have approached the spiritual path with an element of righteousness and teachers came along who really helped us a lot with it. The teacher who helped me most about my righteousness probably was Chögyam Trungpa Rinpoche. What you look for in a really good teacher is that quality of rascality, not a scoundrel but a rascal. I remember when I was teaching at Naropa. That first summer, when Naropa started, I was having a hard time with Trungpa. One of the problems was that he had all of his students drunk most of the time, gambling, and eating heavy meat diets. I thought, What kind of a spiritual teacher is this? You can understand my dilemma. I came out of a Hindu renunciate path and here he was taking them down the path to hell as far as I was concerned, and I was judging. Oh boy, was I judging!

When I looked at those same students a few years later, I saw students deep in the hundred thousand prostrations, deep in the heaviest spiritual practices, because Trungpa had taken them through their obsessions and then on to deeper practices. He wasn't afraid to do that. Most other traditions are afraid of getting lost along the way. But that's what a true tantric teacher is not afraid to do. Tantrics are very exciting and very scary, and you never know whether the tantric is just hung up on themselves or whether they're an exquisite teacher. And there's no way you can know. Were Rajneesh's ninety-two Rolls-Royces a spiritual ploy or was he really a hung-up Indian? You just don't know.

All you have to know is that if you want to be free, you work with these teachers as hard as you can to be free. Their karmic problems are their karmic problems. And that's the secret you finally find out about teachers.

Chapter 10

The Community of Spiritual Seekers

In Buddhism, a practitioner takes refuge in the Triple Gem: first in the Buddha, the fully enlightened one; then in the dharma, the teachings given by the Buddha; and finally in the sangha, the spiritual community. The sangha is both "noble" and "ordinary." The noble sangha includes bodhisattvas, arhats, and the lineage of sages and wisdom holders. The ordinary sangha or satsang, as the community is called in Hinduism, is where "the rubber meets the road."

For unenlightened beings, problems naturally arise. There's competition (we used to call it the "grace race") and anger and jealousy. Ram Dass used to describe the workings of satsang as the "sandpaper effect"—smoothing down our ragged edges through our conflicts and confrontations with one another. And our love. These are the people with whom we share our struggles and our spiritual goals. These are the people who are there for us in our dark night of the soul, in the difficulties we encounter with teachers and methods. These are the friends who offer a hug when we are crying, either in pain or in bliss, and a hand to hold when we feel alone on our paths. Without satsang, it would be a lonely path indeed. As Thich Nhat Hanh said, "We have to take refuge in our sangha, our community of practice. We cannot continue our practice very long without a sangha. . . . We all need a sangha very much."

Once you acknowledge that you are on a journey into a spiritual awareness and perspective about life, then you say, "Who will I hang out with who will help me?" So you listen to hear whom you work with. You can surround yourself with books—the teachings of so and so, or quotes, or the sayings of Christ, or Rumi or Kabir—which I do. I always have a few of them in my bag or in the car and I'll read a shloka, maybe three or four lines, and then let it work on me. It's like fortune cookies; it's got to be a positive message.

Then you begin to see what it is to be with living satsang as opposed to books. You begin to appreciate the value of comparing maps along the way on the journey, seeing who's where. Sometimes you can find those people and sometimes you can't. As you need them more, you start to be tuned to those variables in other people instead of being attracted to them because of something else. You are attracted because there's somebody who would be nice to spend time with around the journey. I find that many people have a hard time getting into it with another person about spiritual work because it's not a socially easy thing. You sort of laugh and kid and it's hard to really go in. I like when it is acceptable social policy to go in.

In our relationships with each other, we begin to see how much we get trapped in the kinds of things that make us into objects for each other instead of subject. And we start to see this is a kind of a curriculum for us to break through the subject-object relationship with another human being. Now, sometimes, if you're lucky, you find other human beings who want to break through it with you. That's what the sangha is about. It's the community of beings who say, "Let's be together in order to awaken out of the illusion of our separateness." It's a spiritual community where you are lucky enough to have a partner who says, "Let's use our relationship in order to awaken and let's use it in order to get free of the traps of our own minds so that we can really be together in truth behind the dramas, behind the symbology, so we can be together as the spirit behind the form."

Very often you can form groups where there is a conscious intention to use the process of the group to awaken. That's a very interesting kind of group to form. You form groups around bowling, around your children, you form groups around mah-jongg or crocheting. You find groups around mountain climbing or cooking together or around athletic events. It's interesting to form a group around becoming conscious. You sit down and say, "Well, how will we do it?" And then everybody throws in their ideas and you practice different things.

I have a wonderful group of around eight of us in this area and we meet once a month. When we meet, a person shares their practice with the others and takes them into it and explores it. Then we discuss it and then we meditate together. It's as simple as that. It's been going on for a year and a half now and it tastes good. It feels good. It feels like a useful device, but it takes initiative. It takes a willingness to say, "My life has a significant component of awakening and I would like to start to select out of the universe those things that can help me awaken."

As you begin to see where you're going with human relationships, and you want to awaken out of your own separateness and your own isolation, to the extent you have a choice, you are going to look for people who will want to enter into some contract to awaken through truth and sharing. See, the ideal relationship is where you and I collaborate to come to truth together. We consciously collaborate, and we enter into the community of other beings who don't think you're nuts for having this other level of consciousness. It's the group where you and I agree that I'll help you awaken if you'll help me awaken. That's an ideal relationship.

It's an incredibly exciting adventure for human relationships and it's the most profound yoga that I know of. It's also the hardest one because it keeps the relationship right on the fine line between chaos and cosmos. It's not a secure thing. You can't settle in and say, "Well, you're always this way." Because the person may not be that. And one of the criteria for being in a relationship in which you're trying to use it to awaken is the simple rule of truth.

Truth

Truth is not a concept. As you move consciousness through planes of awareness, you see that things are *relatively real*. They're real and true within a subsystem. When I was going through college, I was taught Newtonian physics as if it were absolutely real. That's how old I am. Then along came relativity, Einstein's theory, and if you read the books now, Newtonian physics is taught entirely differently. It is a beautiful description of a subsystem. Under these conditions, this will apply. Well, it's the same with conceptual truth. It applies on different planes and the truth is the unity of things.

What you know is relative truth, not absolute truth. Absolute truth has no concept. But there are relative truths and you keep using the relative truths to climb toward the absolute truth, not holding on to them too tightly and getting rigid about them. If I said to you, "What is this moment?" there is no conceptual structure answer. If you wrote poetry, like Shelley and Keats and Byron, and just wrote and wrote and wrote, you wouldn't begin to approximate what truth is. The feeling of the air on your cheek. The light, the shadow, the gathering of people, the consciousness. The fullness of the truth of this moment, there's no way to conceive of it. One just keeps moving toward it all the time.

Maharajji said, "Tell the truth." The next day he'd say, "Love everybody." And the truth was I didn't love everybody. I didn't know why he said to tell the truth. Was my behavior untruthful? I covered stuff over with a lot of wise-guy words. He asked me to tell the truth and I said, "Oh, I do." That's a lie. I was always trying to wise guy it. I didn't like the truth game because I was a homosexual. I was always living double lives and double-double-double lives. In my lectures, I'm honest about my life, but the only thing I don't talk about is homosexuality. My homosexuality is the only thing I wasn't truly candid about. I wouldn't lie, but I wouldn't tell the truth about that. I didn't share my truth because I couldn't be true about it, and that's why I felt like a phony in lectures. And everybody's going, "Oh, you're so honest."

Maharajji said: "Total truth is necessary. You must live

by what you say. Truth is the most difficult tapasya [discipline]. Men will hate you for telling the truth. They will call you names. They may even kill you, but you must tell the truth. Christ died for the truth. If you live in truth, God will always stand with you."

When we asked Maharajji how the heart could be purified, he said, "Always speak the truth." Truth is heavy to deal with in human relationships, as is sitting down with another human being and sharing your truth. See, in most contracts between human beings, truth is not required. What is required is you don't say things that will hurt them. You don't say things that will upset them.

Satsang in Sanskrit means "the company of truth." In satsang, you allow people to be who they are. There is a way in which I say, "Look, I am who I am. Let's enter into this contract in which we will be straight with each other." I've sat with people and I'll tell you how scary and far out it can get. You sit with somebody and you face them for about five hours. I've done this with husbands and wives and all kinds of people. You take turns. You ask, "If there is anything you can bring to mind that would be difficult or uncomfortable to share with me, share it now." Just feel the pain of that thought. Think of what that brings to mind. Oh my God, no, I'm not going to tell her that! Just that question brings forth all the stuff in your mind that you wouldn't want to share with another human being.

Everybody's got their stuff. It is not the stuff itself; it is the fear of sharing it that cuts you off from another human being. When I have a thought that I can't tell you, what happens is a little part of my mind makes you object. It keeps you at a distance from me. I find after a while that if I really want to enter into a relationship of living truth, I can't afford the lie any longer. It's costing too much. Every one of those lies deadens the relationship. It only takes a little bit of lying and it makes the relationship a little deader, a little deader, a little deader, because it's the part where the other person is object.

I've watched relationships where people start to talk and share this stuff. I was a therapist for years, so I've heard it all. I mean, what are you going to tell somebody? I masturbate. I had sex with somebody else. I want to kill you. I'm thinking of eating you alive. I pick my nose. I have these weird sexual fantasies. What could it be? It's stuff. It's all stuff.

You've got to realize that a relationship based on truth is going to always walk the fine line between cosmos and chaos. It's not that you can say, "Well, you're always who you are and I'm always who I am" because we're constantly changing. And that's living spirit. That's living truth. Most people can't stand that. They want to settle for and live a half-truth. I don't want to say to you that I can't stand you in this moment, because you couldn't handle it. So out of kindness for you, I won't tell you the truth. And out of that kind of kindness, what happens is people go into deadness in their relationship. They're not alive.

A lot of people settle for that in relationships because their relationship isn't their vehicle for awakening. It's just a secure thing on the back burner. But if you're going to make a relationship into a vehicle for awakening, then it has to evolve. If the other partner doesn't want to play, you'll find someone else who will play. Others stay right in it and just keep working with it, not demanding the other person awaken. You have no real right to ask another person to awaken. What you do is your work on yourself.

Truth or Honesty?

The question is, Are we talking about truth or honesty? Truth is about the facts, while honesty is about expressing your feelings and thoughts accurately. If you're honest, you don't tell lies or spread rumors about other people; you admit your mistakes even if it gets you in trouble. I think I would rather say, "Let us be honest with one another." In a way we are cutting through the conceptual structures that are keeping us from being together in truth, which is the nonconceptual way of being together. Gandhi's autobiography was called *The Story of My Experiments with Truth*—experiments of learning how to move toward truth by honesty as a vehicle. By sharing, sharing, but sharing honestly.

When you look around at your relationships, you will see how few of your relationships have this contractual agreement. The contractual agreement is: I won't bug you, you don't bug me. I have my privacy, you have your privacy. It's all wonderful, it works, it's efficient, but you end up alone. If you're going to use relationships to break out of the alienated state, it's a scary business, but the reward of it is incredible.

The board for the Seva Foundation is a type of satsang. The Seva Foundation is a very interesting experiment.* There are eighteen of us on the board, made up of doctors and professors and all kinds of people, some from India, some from the States. Our summer board meeting goes on for seven days. The first day is a day of meditation in which we all quiet down

* Seva is going stronger than ever these days. Visit https://www.seva.org.

and get here. We do some practices, some meditative practices. Then we start the process of "circle sharing" the next day. We start going around the circle, each person bringing everybody up to date about what's happening in their lives. My children, what's happening in my family, what's happening in my work, et cetera.

Then we start going around deeper. What are the things that are keeping me stuck at this moment? And it gets interesting. Then as we go around the circle, what is it about anybody else in this group that is catching me. See? For example, we got a committee together but you didn't ever call a meeting and you really screwed up that committee. Do I tell you that or don't I tell you that? Or, you know, you always come off sort of half-cocked; you don't really know what you're talking about. Or you went to Guatemala and then you made a statement in the press that has caused some real problems for us and we don't think we should trust you to go to Guatemala. These are our fellow board members. We begin to see that for the board to be the center of a powerful organization, we have to set the criteria that we are going to be straight and clear with each other.

Now, there are very few boards that any of you have ever been on that have demanded that kind of criteria. Usually everybody comes in as an expert, everybody leaves each other's territory alone, and the result is you come to a board meeting, you serve, you feel like you're a good guy, you go away, but you didn't get fed by the process. At Seva, we come out of those board meetings much more vibrant and alive. We take breaks to play volleyball every few hours so we won't get lost in the shuffle, and we shift our game of who we are at that moment. It's kind of an experiment of an intentional community that comes together in order to awaken. We're coming together in order to awaken through doing service.

I was on tour in Washington, DC, when I was asked to visit a fellow who had very severe AIDS symptoms. He had a fever and had candida throughout his whole mouth, esophagus, stomach, et cetera. And he was a very, very beautiful young guy. He had been a needle user and had become clean eight years previously, but he had been infected by that time. Now he was really, really pissed off. He was miserable; he was in pain. He was angry at the doctors because they wouldn't give him enough pain medication. He was so miserable he didn't want to go on living, but the year before he had converted to Catholicism so he couldn't kill himself. So he was in an interesting situation when I got there.

I sat down on the bed, took his hand, and listened as he went through this incredible anger, sadness, feeling of loss, self-pity, et cetera. I was completely in it with him. I was suggesting other doctors he might meet and talking about how he might deal with his mother. We were in the world of stuff and we were doing it together. I was upset when he was upset. I had the additional upset of being happy I wasn't in his predicament and all the guilt that brings up.

After about forty-five minutes, he quieted down enough from emitting this stuff so that there were little spaces of silence in the room. Slowly our eyes met, and there was the flickering of the eyes and then the quieting of the eyes and then we were just sitting here together. In the next few minutes, the place in which we were sitting together became real and all of the stuff—the thems and thats and this pain and nice man come to visit and all that stuff—became phenomena on the ocean of awareness. He and I had entered into an incredibly intimate space of shared awareness. That's real intimacy. You're sharing the same space and time at the same moment together. For the next hour we sort of danced about life and death and silence and play and stayed in this space of shared awareness together.

When I left, we were both in an ecstatic state. Now I had the interesting challenge of getting in my car and driving on the freeway and he had the interesting challenge of coming back to being somebody with AIDS symptoms, but it seemed to me, when I thought about it, that he and I had served each other well.

So many of the fears of this and that arise out of such a deep sense of alienation, of being separate and alone. We stayed in close enough, long enough, to get through the reactive drama between us in order to recognize our existence and recognize the context in which all the phenomena are occurring. It's a great gift to be able to share with another human being. In fact, that's the essence of helping. It's like saying to another heart, "You are not alone. Here we are. Maybe we can't do anything except just be together, but maybe in the being together all that will seem different."

Celebrating Satsang

One day I was in South India in Madras, and I was with an older Indian man (*hmm*, my age). He said, "Would you like to celebrate my birthday with me?" He was a devotee of my guru. I said yes. He said, "Why don't you be outside your hotel tomorrow morning at seven thirty?" It's hard to imagine what birthday you celebrate at seven thirty in the morning, but I'm game.

I'm outside the next morning and his Ambassador pulls up, the Indian car. And in it are the man and his wife, his daughter and son-in-law, and his son and daughter-in-law. Of course there's room for me because it's an Indian car. So I get in and we all drive. Nobody says a word to me. Good morning, beautiful day, nice mist. We're just driving somewhere for something. I love the mystery of the universe. I don't have to know everything.

At one point he pulls up to some gates and they open and he drives into a courtyard. I look around and there must be two hundred people standing there, each holding a tin plate. Some of them are old, some of them look quite mad. They're all indigent. The car stops right in the middle of the courtyard. The man gets out of the car and opens the trunk. There are these huge cauldrons of cooked food. He hands each of us a pail and a ladle. We fill up the pails and then go up and down the lines to give everybody food. Within twenty minutes, all the food is gone and all the people are fed. The pots are empty. We put the pails in the pots, close the trunk, get into the car, and drive out of the ashram.

We get outside and he says to me, "Now that was a birthday!"

Chapter 11

God, Guru, Self

God, guru, self—the holy trinity, the three-in-one. Pick a path along any of the three lines and you will reach the same destination. More consciousness. More clarity. More peace. More love. They are all doorways leading to the inner sanctum, to the merging with the One. And as Ramana Maharshi so succinctly said, "There is no difference between God, Guru, and Self."

When a girl who was with my guru was having trouble with a rather fickle boyfriend, Maharajji said to her, "Don't you realize your only friend is God?" Now, I realize the word "God" makes a lot of people wince or tighten. There are some of you for whom the word "God" is a real no-no. It comes out of your childhood and a lot of unpleasant experiences you've had with that concept. It also comes out of your fear that you're going to get caught in dualism, in worshipping something external to yourself.

When I say the word "God," if I make it clear what I think, I don't have to wince when I say it. When I use the word "God," I don't anthropomorphize. When I use the word "God," I am not thinking of the Old Testament grandfatherly figure with a stern visage; I'm experiencing God. I see God as all form and as the formless made manifest into all this form. I am talking about that vastness of myself that is below the surface, the iceberg. We're talking about the part that I don't know of myself, that deepest part of my being, my god-self. In Hinduism, they call it the *atman*, that part of God that's within oneself.

In devotional yoga, when you sing Torah or you sing to Krishna or you talk to Christ, you are anthropomorphizing that quality we call God. That's okay because it opens your heart and directs it toward somebody, and then you go through that somebody into that which is beyond. It is taking your emotional body with you rather than leaving your emotional body behind. That's all I can understand.

For me God is a concept; it's like a finger pointing at the moon. It's not the finger. It isn't the moon. The word "God" has nothing to do with it. "God" is a short word for labeling that which is unspeakable. The Hebrews, realizing that, spell it G-D. It's an unspeakable word. It's not unspeakable because it's so secret; it's unspeakable because no word can contain what it is.

Before the first manifestation into dualism and into polarities of positive and negative, yin and yang, you go back into formlessness where nothing has yet manifested. In that space, everything is in its imminent form, not in its manifest form. At that point you are closest to what might be called "absolute truth," because the minute it comes into dualism, it is all only relatively true from then on. All of the manifestation into form is merely the other side of the coin of the unmanifest. It's all sitting there in the unmanifest.

God is not a somebody or a something you can grasp. But you can use the concept of God to go beyond the concept of God. You can use the One to get rid of your two-ness.

When you start to appreciate that God is everywhere, or spirit is everywhere, then the question comes: Why aren't I seeing it? Then you realize it's in the eyes of the beholder. It's at which level you are choosing to look or at which level your desires are allowing you to look. If you're hungry, you just see what's edible. It's only when you start to yearn to know your true self or yearn to see beyond or realize the ephemeral nature of all the stuff that you grab hold of in the world that you start to turn your direction toward God.

The Guru

Saying that God, guru, and self are one is a very profound statement. It means that your path may take you toward God or to the edge of formlessness or to the One. You may think about it, talk about it, sing about it, do service to it. One person may do it with a guru, with a form that is the doorway into that thing. Another person feels it's most valid to do it inwardly, to meet the guru inside, which is the same thing. You meet exactly the same thing whichever way you go. They are just different strokes for different folks.

I have my guru, who's not in his body anymore but still teaches me from another plane. At times I have hated him, and my intellect has said he is a total phony, a charlatan exploiting me. My mind has done all kinds of stuff about him, but that inner voice says, "Go, baby, go. This is the pure thing." And if you are like me, you are totally hooked on purity. You are looking for that pure light, even when that purity comes in strange forms.

Don't confuse purity and righteousness. They're not the same thing. Purity is the cleanliness of the feeling of the presence of the living spirit. It's not goody-goody. Cleanness, clarity, and a kind of a love that's like a diamond love. It's not a thick saccharin-type love. With such a being, when they're really clear, no matter how deep in you go, you won't find them. Only when you know your self will you know them.

Believe me, when you have raised your hand in purity and said, "Hey, God, recognize me. I'm coming" . . . that reaching forth is what calls forth the grace. You may have many teachers on the physical plane, but your guru may not be on the physical plane at all. Your guru may be Christ, or Krishna, or any number of beings, but the minute you raise your hand, your satguru recognizes you. It's really much less important that you know your guru than your guru knows you.

By now I have some understanding that love is the presence. That's when I sit and bring Maharajji here. I can sit with pictures of him and remember the form, and then I can sit with the feeling of his presence in the room, like you're in a dark room and somebody's in there but you can't see them. His presence to me is very much love and is the essence of the witness, the nonjudgmental love. It's a feeling of I'm home at last. Home at last.

I actively bring Maharajji into my reflections on all things. Here's what I do. I feel the presence, like a presence in the room. Once I feel that presence, I shift to my imagination and I imagine he's actually there in the room. I imagine him talking to me. I realize that he's in control of my imagination. When people say, "You're talking to your dead guru. It's your imagination," I say, "That's exactly what it is."

Then if I keep getting quieter and quieter, which now and then happens, it's as if there's a merging, not that he becomes me or I become him but that we become *it*. The identity of the forms dissolves. It's like all of this stuff keeps dissolving into awareness.

Guru Kripa

My basic method is what's called *guru kripa*, which means "the grace of the guru." Even though I do Buddhist meditation and I do Sufi dance and I am involved with Hanuman, the monkey god, and Hinduism, even though I love Christ and study kabbalah, beyond all that, I am continuously in dialogue with Maharajji, Neem Karoli Baba. I've gone from relating to that historical person—a man in a blanket in India—to relating to the qualities of that being. Everything I'm doing is a dialogue with him. It's as if I'm experiencing him constantly in manifestation. Only a few times have I seen him in dreams or visions, where he's come and manifested and said something to me. But that's very rare. I don't get much of that stuff.

What a guru does is mirror for you where you aren't. That's all they do. But we took that whole concept of guru and turned it into our need for a good father, in a psychodynamic sense; we wanted the guru to do it *to* us. In fact, what happens is that the guru just *is*, like a tree or a river. And depending on your karmic predispositions or readiness, you do it to yourself. The guru is a presence that allows you to do it. It's a presence that doesn't catch you anywhere. Only you catch yourself.

Each night, Buddha would look out over all the Buddha realms, at all the realms of existence, not just this plane, but all the realms, to see who was ready for that touch or that connection or that grace. For one thought of the guru, when you are ready, will liberate. But nothing will happen if you're not ready. A guru who is a true guru just is, and you take what you need. The very existence of the guru is grace. They won't come and take on your karma just like that. But if you give them your karma, then it will go through them, and you will be free of it.

As I look around at people, my sense is that they are receiving teachings just about as fast as they are ready, one way or another. They receive the teachings inside, through their inner light, through visions, through dreams. I get hundreds of letters from people who read *Miracle of Love*. They say, "Maharajji came to me after I read the book." So they've got him as much as I've got him, and he's guiding them as much as he's guiding me. They say, "Yeah, but you had Maharajji in form." But it turns out that once he comes to you, either he's there or he isn't there. Once people trust those kinds of ways of being with spiritual guides, or inner messages, or things like that, they're getting everything they need.

Your Inner Voice

How can you be sure that the inner voice you hear is the true one, the clear connection to God? The answer is, you can't. In fact, that's why Quakers call it the "still, small voice" within. And there are all these other voices, which are your desires masquerading as God. They're saying, "I'm God, listen to me." Get as much as you can. You'll listen and you'll listen and you'll hear a message, and you'll start a journey, and it won't click.

You'll learn to use this image of *clicking*. It doesn't click, it doesn't feel right. Something that is in harmony in the universe is in harmony on every level of reality. You'll find you're doing something which is beautiful at one level and stinks at another level. It won't click; it'll feel off. You've got to start to trust that process. You keep tuning and tuning to that inner voice and tuning and tuning and tuning, and the more you quiet your mind, and the freer you get of the clinging to thought forms, the more you will hear that voice, because it's not a voice of the intellect. It's much deeper. It's what we in the West sometimes call an "intuitive voice," but it's even deeper than that.

Quiet your mind and sit down and follow your breath. Just follow the breath in and out of your nostrils for twenty minutes. At the end of twenty minutes, you're in a much better space to hear your inner voice than you were before. You're quieter, your mind is quieter, and the more your heart is open to the flow, the more you're flowing, and the quieter your mind, the clearer that inner voice will get. So this is a process of tuning yourself as a receiver, to hear right.

Many times you'll hear the wrong voice, you'll act on it and it won't click, and you'll stop. You'll say, "I blew it again." If you had done it perfectly and could hear that voice perfectly and always did the right thing, you'd be enlightened. There'd be nothing to do. So the journey to enlightenment is the journey of errors. You should use your mistakes and respect them as symptoms or information about the unique predilections or predispositions your journey is taking. If I feel no, that isn't my way—even if everybody else says it is the way—I trust that feeling in myself. I keep readjusting to find what route is appropriate for me.

Maybe you don't yet trust your inner voice enough to guide you, and you are seeking a true guru. That's just another strategy for life. The means is the journey itself as well as the end. Going for the guru is reaching for truth, the aspiring toward truth. That is what the journey is about. That aspiring will allow you to look at everybody and say, "Are you the guru?" After a while, instead of "No, you're not the guru," and becoming a connoisseur of clay feet, you get to the point where you start to look through the veil and see that everybody, in fact, is the guru in drag.

Whole in One

As I moved into the mid-sixties of my life, I realized I needed to get more exercise and so the first thing I tried was Gold's Gym. There were all these people with huge pecs and lats and they'd walk around like gorilla world. I began to think I was like these guys. I had a trainer. One day she had just put me through a very intense exercise routine and I was sitting there deciding whether to live or die. She said, "Is everything all right?" I knew she wouldn't have asked one of them. At that moment I knew I wasn't one of them.

I wanted to find something that would get me outside a little more, so I decided to take up golf again, which I had played when I was very young. I was lousy then and I'm lousy now. So I started to take lessons and became a very gung-ho golfer. My consciousness had changed so much from when I had played golf as a teenager that I immediately saw that golf was a total mind game. Where was your consciousness when you brought the club back and swung it through? And I saw that it was no different from following my breath. So I'd walk up to the ball and I'd do a meditative thing, and the ball would do its thing, and then I would walk, getting exercise and enjoying nature. I'd come up to the next hole and I'd do a meditative thing. I'd meditate, walk, meditate, walk, meditate, walk. And my golf game improved immensely.

Pretty soon my teacher and I had become playing buddies, and I was traveling down to Palm Springs to play all the fancy golf courses with threesomes and foursomes. Every afternoon I'd go out to play, and I'd be paired up with people, and they'd always be sort of retired Republicans. "Hello, I'm Fred." And I'd say, "Hello, I'm Dick." Every now and then at the golf course somebody would come up and say, "Ram Dass??? WHAT are you DOING HERE??" It's like you'd just been caught at some terribly perverse occupation. I'd say, "I'm playing golf!"

A book came out in the sixties called *Golf in the Kingdom*, by Mike Murphy, who started Esalen. The main character was Shivas Irons, a kind of a mystic who taught golf. It became an underground cult book and an organization was started called the Shivas Irons Society, made up of mystical golfers. They heard that I was golfing, so they invited me to give the keynote address at their conference at Stanford. I did, and now that tape is like one of the hot tapes on the golf market! (That tape became a podcast episode on the Be Here Now Network.*)

What's interesting about that to me is that I've gotten now to the point that I see that human beings are human beings, and my situation brings me in contact with human beings for a lot of different reasons. Sometimes it's at the checkout counter at the supermarket. Sometimes it's somebody I'm playing golf with on the golf course. Sometimes it's somebody in the business community I'm working with. And I realize that when I get rid of my models about who you are, and my models about who I am, and allow this to be an interaction, it all comes alive. I find I get fed incredibly by human relationships and come away feeling very enriched. I'm not trapped in the kind of narrow "We play golf together." We are souls who happen to be playing golf together.

---

* Ram Das, host, *Here and Now*, podcast, episode 267, "The Mystical Nature of Golf," Be Here Now Network, https://beherenownetwork.com/ram-dass-here-and-now-ep-267-the-mystical-nature-of-golf/.

Recently I played with the meanest, most unhappy guy. Every shot he took he swore. He actually threw his club by the second hole. I turned to him and said, "You having fun?" I had encroached upon his privacy.

He said, "YES!"

And I said, "Good! I just wanted to make sure you're having fun. Enjoy yourself!"

By the end of the round he said, "I don't know who you are, but could we play together again?"

It is such fun to dance in the forms of life. To me, he was my guru in drag, saying, "I bet you won't find me in this one!"

Chapter 12

Wholeness and Loving Awareness

What it comes down to, always, is love. Beyond romantic love, beyond the love of your kids and your pets and your best friend, beyond the love of the stars and the moon, is the love that is. The path of the heart, bhakti yoga, is the union with the all *that comes through love and devotion. But it's still a path, with all the pitfalls and obstacles of any path.*

For more than five decades, Ram Dass opened many possible doorways for us to follow as we stumble along on our way to the recognition of God, guru, and self. He plunged into various techniques, absorbed teachings from different traditions, and always kept Maharajji as his guiding light. In the years that followed his debilitating stroke, he dove deeper and deeper into his being and wound up with the teaching that was closest to his realization of how it all is: I am loving awareness. *Loving awareness: the coming together of love and consciousness, the grace-full culmination of all he had learned and wanted to teach.*

The spiritual path is a graceful opportunity for us. The fact that you and I even hear there is such a path is grace for a human life, from a karmic point of view. In a way, what the spiritual path offers is a chance for us to come back into the innate, compassionate quality of our heart and our intuitive wisdom. We can get back into the balance where, when we need our intellect, it's available as a servant, but we are not ruled by it and trapped in our thinking mind. To me, that is well worth working toward. Most of the social, ecological, and political problems we have are the creation of the human intellect, along with all its benefits. The answer to that is the recognition of the unitive nature of all things and realizing you are nothing and therefore you are everything.

Each of us must be true to ourselves to hear *what is our unique way through*. Because if you get phony holy, it ends up kicking you in the butt. You've got to stay true to yourself. The art form of the whole dance is to be born into separateness, to grow and learn in your separateness. You've got to get caught in it, and then at some point to awaken to the fact that you aren't who you thought you were. As Buddha indicated with his term *anatta*, there is no permanent unchanging self. There are just sets of phenomena happening. Don't take yourself so seriously. Don't get hung up on who you think you are and how you think it should come out, what you think is bad and what you think is good.

Can you live outside of time and still dance within time? Can you be free of the fear of annihilation and still be an instrument for the healing of the world? Will you become a better one if you are not doing it out of fear but doing it out of celebratory joy and love?

If you want to live on a healing planet, become that which you would do, not out of trying but of opening into, of listening your way into the Tao, into the wisdom of the elders. If you want to live in a conscious environment, the game is basically to become a conscious person.

Making All Things New

As you extricate yourself from patterns of thought, you look at everything freshly. Look, I am making all things new. It's all emerging and it's all very precious and very beautiful. We get so caught in the habits of mind we can't look freshly. We don't have rituals of transformation so we can look with new eyes. My bar mitzvah wasn't that for me; it didn't bring me back into the blend of the two planes of consciousness, the formless and the form.

In Aldous Huxley's *Island*, he had an initiation rite which used the moksha (liberation) medicine and various trials. We, however, have not invested in rituals that allow us to affirm the beauty of what is natural to us all the time—rituals around stages of life, rituals around changes in nature like solstices, rituals around fertility, rituals around harvest, rituals around eating, rituals around resting, rituals around planets, rituals around gathering together. We don't invest in making life sacred. We keep profaning it into our own greed of I want that, I desire that.

The predicament with rituals is that a technique for awakening you to the freshness in one moment, a moment later is an institution that puts you to sleep. It's lost its juice. As Gurdjieff [a Greek philosopher, mystic, and spiritual teacher] said, "An alarm clock that wakes you one moment, you can sleep right through later on."* Most of the rituals that we now find abhorrent were at one time rituals that awakened people.

Really what's required is you have to keep recreating them over and over again. It involves slowing down. That's part of why we use poetry and art, because they remind us of the appreciation of the simplest things, like a bowl of fruit or light coming through a windowpane. What Matisse or Gauguin could do to remind us is quite incredible. Poets and artists appreciate the fullness of the moment.

The Path of the Heart

Like the fragrance of orchids, the path of love—the path of emotion, the path of the heart—takes you to the essence of love; it takes you from loving to *being love*. Like all paths, it is fraught with pitfalls and traps. Most of our emotions either are in the service of our minds or are frightening things that overwhelm us and make us afraid. So we protect ourselves and thus come through life a little bit like hungry ghosts.

We are beings with a huge need for love, but it's like we have some kind of amoeba that doesn't allow us to digest our food. So though we get love, it goes through us and then we need love

* Commonly ascribed to Gurdjieff

all over again. It's so deep in all of us that we've built a whole reality around it and we think that's the way it is—that everybody needs love and that if you don't get it, you are deprived. The more of it, the better. And you need it every day. It's like an achievement. You see, the minute people achieve something, it becomes irrelevant and their awareness turns to the next achievement. They're addicted to the practice, not to the goal.

If you are cut off in your heart from love, you feel hungry. That hunger is the hunger to come home. It's the hunger to be at peace, to be feeling at one. In the universe where lover and beloved merge, it's the place to feel fulfilled, fully in the moment, and whole.

There are a set of factors in you that are like a lock waiting for a key to open to love. But the key must fit into that lock. It must be a certain pattern or concatenation of factors. The fact that I could open up to my guru I am sure had something to do with my relationship to my father. You think, Well, spirit is spirit and psychological is psychological. But all of your psychological conditioning prepares you to be attracted to certain methods or to certain paths or to certain people.

You are like a bee looking for a flower. You're flying around buzzing, just looking. For many people, at the time they are seeking love so strongly, these are second-chakra energies—energies of sexual desire, of desire for union that is relational—and the energy gets into that pattern and you associate "making love" as a vehicle to coming into love.

So you're going along like a little lock waiting for a key. A shadow of lover goes by and like a little duckling you turn and start to walk after it. It just happened to be the particular pattern that turned you on, that opened you up. You say, "I think

I'm in love with him or with her," not "I think I'm in love"—I think I'm in love *with her* or *with him*. And if you're lucky, your key unlocks her or his lock and his or her key unlocks your lock. You love me, I love you. Here we are. Through this dynamic, you have opened to the place that's feeding the unity space behind the dualism. You say, "I am in love with you; you are the key stimulus that is opening me to the place in myself where I am love, which I can't get to except through you." Imagine if you've been going around like a hungry ghost, starving for love, and you suddenly meet somebody who opens you to this reservoir, this ocean of love, this ocean of feeling at home. You're so happy!

If you meet a master and the master shares with you a method and the method works to tune you to the place in yourself of awareness of love, you end up loving that method and you love that master. You get really drunk on it and very addicted to it. The method that opens you when you're hungry for love is usually another person. You get very attached or addicted to being in the presence of that other person, and then starts the fear—the fear that that person is going to die or leave you or won't be around. Then you get jealous and possessive and you keep creating a hell realm around the addiction to your vehicle for coming to love, getting so caught in a relationship that you can't ever arrive at the essence of dwelling in love.

The spiritual practice of devotion is designed to move you from "I love you" to "We are in love together." Now, consider love as a huge hot tub, which is a very personal image for me. Let us get into the hot tub. Together we are meeting in the space of love. When two people meet in the space of love and break the attachment of mind to seeing the other person as the vehicle to get you there—but realize that it's in you, and you start through your spiritual practices to rest in it—suddenly the need and desperation start to dissolve. All of the negative things start to disappear—the possessiveness, the jealousy, the anger, the fear that the other person's going to die—because the quality of love as a state has no time. It has no space. It wasn't born and it doesn't die.

We get caught in our separateness. We are hungry for the coming back into love, of the merging place, the namaste place, the place where when you are in yours and I'm in mine, we are in love together. We are in a place where your heart-mind and my heart-mind remain always inseparable.

There are a variety of ways in which the heart path works. In Hinduism, they spell them out. There is the relationship between mother and child, for example, between Mary and Jesus. There is the relationship of friends, like between John and Jesus. There is the relationship of disciple to master, and the relationship of servant to master. There is the relationship of father and child. There is the relationship of lover and beloved. Ultimately you will find that, because of your unique set of patternings, one of those forms will feel most attractive to you. You will explore them all, but one of them will feel most attractive.

What I find is that all those ways have become my way. Everywhere I look, I see my beloved. I don't see the form as a historical form or as a special form. It's as if this is all God and every one of you is my guru come in drag to catch me. The quality of my guru was that he was nobody special. He was just another being. There was nobody there, but every time you looked at him, you just fell in love.

On the path of devotion, you get so addicted to that experience of that intimacy between the lover and the beloved that you keep being drawn into the singing and the stories and the images and the remembrance of, and you're just thinking about it and tuning all the time to stay in that intimate, loving relationship with that which you love. Then there's this little shift where you start to ask the question, What isn't God? You start to look at all the different faces and aspects and watch your heart close around judgment; you practice opening your heart and looking and loving this as a manifestation of the beloved. Then the love starts to get vast.

Kabir said:

> Since the day when I met with my Lord, there has been no end to the sport of our love.
> I shut not my eyes, I close not my ears, I do not mortify my body;
> I see with eyes open and smile, and behold His beauty everywhere:
> I utter His Name, and whatever I see, it reminds me of Him; whatever I do, it becomes His worship.

Loving Everyone

The cultural models of romantic love have to do with specialness. I love you specially. What I experience is that I don't love people specially. I have special work to do with one person or another, but I'm getting to love the universe and I'm getting to love the manifestation. It's interesting because people keep wanting you to love them specially and I don't feel it anymore.

I'll tell you what happened to me. I started to guide people through acid trips back in the sixties. I'd take acid with them and we'd both go into the place of merging. We were in love. And then the session would be over, and we'd be parting in the beautiful morning mist and they would say, "When can I see you again?" Imagine. I mean you've just been with somebody in total love and you're about to part; this is where the fear comes in and the lack of faith and the doubt. When will I see you again? I'd say, "Well, why don't we have dinner Wednesday night?" And then it became like every Wednesday night we'd have dinner because that's what you do with a beloved. Let's hang out. Then I ran a second session and the next day the person said, "When will I see you again?" I said, "Well, how about Thursday night?" After I had run six sessions, I went to my teacher, Tim Leary, and said, "Tim, I don't think I can guide any more sessions. I don't have any more evenings free."

At that point I realized I was going to have to take it up to another level of loving people, where if we have a moment of truth of love together, this is what we've got. The clinging of the mind comes out of the fear that says, "I want to possess it because I may run out of love later." When you leap out of that space, you realize that every time you turn around there is another form of the beloved.

You love people just because they are. You love things because they are. You see the manifestation, the awe, the mystery of the divine in form. When that starts to happen, you still have your old models of possession going. They haven't been burned out yet. So when you love the second person, you want to collect them too. And then the third person, you want to collect them. You fall in love with somebody and you collect feathers and straw and drapes and stuff and build a nest. Then you go to the supermarket for yogurt and beer. You're at the checkout counter and you look into the eyes of the person behind the counter, and it happens again. The eyes are the windows of the soul and you're in love because now you're starting to function from this place. When you're in this place, everybody you look at is your lover. When you are in love, you see love wherever you look. My God, this is great. We are in love and it's the checkout person.

So the question is, Have you considered a ménage à trois? Are you opposed to open marriages? But then what's going to happen? You walk down the street and you look and there's another one. Pretty soon the politics get so complicated, plus the emotions of everybody who thinks they're the special one. You realize you've got to graduate from a deprivation model to an abundance model. And I don't mean that in the kind of cheesy way it's often used—abundance so I can have it all. It's abundant because *you are love.*

As you become love, you get to the point where you walk down the street and somebody comes and is the most beautiful thing that you have ever seen. You look and you look and you appreciate and you love, and your eyes may meet and you both recognize the love . . . and you don't have to do anything about it. You go from "Come live with me" to "Let's have coffee together" to "Would you give me your number?" to "How about a calling card?" to a wink to "Are you experiencing what I'm experiencing? Wasn't this great? God is love," and then you're just looking at your beloved.

It's nothing special to be in love. It's very ordinary. How alien it is in this culture to think that being in love with the universe is ordinary.

What Is Enlightenment?

Enlightenment is like jumping out of a plane and having no parachute. But then you realize there's no earth. It's free form. There are no rules. You are beyond all of it. You *are* all of it. It's just pouring out of you and nothing's happening at all. You're at rest. There's nowhere to stand, so there's no limit to your perspective because you are light. You've merged into the totality of it. The universe is your thought form. This is the way it is.

As Trungpa said in his rascally way, "Enlightenment is the ego's ultimate disappointment." And that's the predicament. You see, the fact is that your spiritual journey is an entirely different ball game from the one you thought you were on. It's very hard to make that transition and a lot of people don't want to. They want to take the power from their spiritual work and make their life nice. That is wonderful and I honor it. It's exactly your karmuppance, but that is not freedom.

What the spiritual path offers as potential is freedom. But freedom demands complete surrender, meaning surrender of who you think you are and what you think you're doing into *what is*, and it's mind-boggling when you understand how powerful is the game of dying into yourself. There is grief when who you thought you were starts to disappear. Kalu Rinpoche said, "We live in illusion, the appearance of things. But there is a reality. We *are* that reality." When you understand this, you see that you are nothing, and being nothing, you are everything. You're everything.

The minute you give up your specialness, you're part of all things. Then you're in harmony, you're in the Tao, you're in the way of things. You're in the moment, but you're not anybody anymore. You're just part of it. This is just phenomena happening at this moment, the illusion that I'm doing this and that you are busy listening; that's all our minds. Behind it, here we are. That is all.

It seems to me that we have two jobs. One is to empty our minds of all the attachments to how we think it ought to come out. And the other is to keep our hearts open. It gets scary when you understand that you're in love with the universe because love is love. It's very open, it's very flowing. It doesn't do well with rules. I remember once I was in an ashram in India and the head of the ashram said to me, "Ram Dass, get up and dance." I was known to dance ecstatically, but ecstatic dance by command is a whole other matter. But I got up and I started to dance and I got more and more ecstatic. In my ecstasy, I crossed over the line in the middle of the hall between the men's section and the women's section because ecstasy is ecstasy. Immediately he stopped the music and the whole thing was over because ecstasy has no place in the ashram rules.

That's one of the predicaments: when you really fall in love, it opens and opens and opens and you don't know where to hold on anymore. You've got to have a lot of trust, a lot of faith. As my friend Mirabai Bush said, "When you feel love, you feel safe in the sense that you've had a glimpse of the interconnection of everything. You've had a glimpse of the sort of fullness and wholeness of who you are and how, even if it's love from one single being, there's a way in which feeling so connected to one being, you can glimpse the way in which you're connected to everything. That sense of safety allows you to let go of some of the things that we need to let go of. Let go of all these ways in which we think of ourselves so that we can get a glimpse and then dwell in who we really are."

Loving Awareness

As your sadhana goes on, as your meditation gets deeper, as you let go of the models of yourself more and more, you begin to touch and enter into that space of love which is the same as consciousness. It's the same place. When you first enter into that space, you begin to experience love toward more and more people. If you have social models about what you do when you're in love with somebody, it gets very complicated because you don't know whom to sleep with first or whom to shake hands with. When you're in love with somebody, you're supposed to at least hug them if not marry them. Finally you just look at each other and you don't do anything because sooner or later you're going to be in love with the universe. You are sitting in the place which is love, which is that channel where it's all one, and when you look at another being, you are looking at love.

When I wake up in the morning, I'm aware of the air, the fan on my ceiling. I've got to love them. I am loving awareness. But if I'm an ego, I'm judging everything as it relates to my own survival. The air might give me a cold that will turn into pneumonia. I'm always afraid of something in the world that I have to defend myself against. If I'm identified with my ego, the ego is frightened because the ego knows that it's going to end at death. But if I merge with love, there's nothing to be afraid of. Loving awareness neutralizes fear.

Loving awareness is the soul. This practice of "I am loving awareness" turns you inward toward the soul. If you dive deep enough into your soul, you will come to God. In Greek, God's love is called *agape*. Martin Luther King Jr. said about agape, this higher love, that it's an overflowing love which is purely spontaneous, unmotivated, groundless, and creative. The love of God operating in the human heart. It's the love Maharajji spreads around—unconditional love. He loves you just because. It's spontaneous, unmotivated, groundless. He's not going to love you because you're an achiever or a devotee or a yogi or because you're on the path. He loves you just because. Can you accept that? Can you accept unconditional love? When you can accept that kind of love, you can give that love. You can give love to all you perceive all the time.

You are love in love with love. You are in the space of love with all beings. It's unbearable at that point because you are still caught in having to do something about it, or you want to collect it because it may get bad later. Ultimately there is a deepening faith and you acknowledge, "I am in the space of love. This is who I am. I have given up all the stuff that's going to pull me out of it." All of the fear in the love relationship is dissipated at that point. You come together with people because it is your dharma to work with them toward going to God.

The ego is up in the head, and my self and Maharajji are down here in the heart. To get from the ego to the big self, I said, "I am loving awareness." This is loving awareness. This is the spiritual heart. I am loving awareness. Loving awareness. I am loving awareness. The awareness you and I know, plus the love that comes from Maharajji. Loving awareness. I am aware of everything. I'm aware of my body. I'm aware of this television, this computer. I am aware of all of it. I am aware, but I notice that I'm loving all of that. I'm loving all of the world, oh boy!

The self that I identify with here is in the ocean of love; the self that lives up here, the ego, it's the ocean of fear, *yech*. Loving awareness. I am aware of what comes in through my ears, eyes, skin. I'm aware of everything outside, but pulling in, pulling into the heart. The spiritual heart brings me to loving awareness. I'm aware of my thoughts. The loving awareness is witnessing my thoughts.

Loving awareness is in the moment. There are past thoughts and there are future thoughts, but you dive deep into the present moment and there you'll find loving awareness. Only this moment is real. The past and the future are all just thoughts. In this moment now, in this spiritual heart, there is peace, there is contentment, there is compassion, there is joy, and there's wisdom. All in your spiritual heart and mine.

Cultivate awareness. To the extent that you are dancing in form, play the most fun game, which is dancing with the beloved. So the earth is the beloved. Your enemies are your beloved. The "other" is the beloved. They are all the face of the beloved, and when you really love somebody, you really, really want them to be happy. It's not a bad gig to just hang out celebrating your beloved. The fact that you're not doing it all the time everywhere must be very hard for you. I wish you Godspeed. It's the journey I'm on. I don't know what else to do in form but dance with the beloved.

Ram Dass's Loving Awareness Meditation

How do you become loving awareness? By identifying with the soul instead of the ego, and then everyone appears like souls to you.

You shift into loving awareness by moving from your head to your spiritual heart. Concentrate on your breath for a moment. In . . . out . . . in . . . out. Maybe the tip of the nose will be the place where you'll do that. Now, move that concentration to the middle of your heart space, the point of loving awareness.

Keep repeating: "I am loving awareness. I am loving awareness. I am loving awareness."

That loving awareness is you. It's the real you. For you are awareness. You can be aware of your eyes and what they see; be aware of the ears and what they hear, be aware of what the skin feels. You can be aware of your mind and the river of thoughts that come out of your mind. Thoughts, thoughts, thoughts. Some of those thoughts are positive, some are negative, some are about you, and some about others. Some of them are judging thoughts. But you will stay identified with loving awareness in your heart, in the heart center.

I am loving awareness. I am loving awareness. I am loving awareness.

Awareness is not a thing. We can label it, but it is not the words. You are loving awareness. So is Christ. So is Krishna. So is Buddha. So is Maharajji. They are loving awareness and so are you. One loving awareness. Each of us is a finger of the hand of loving awareness. Loving awareness is in everybody. Everybody is in loving awareness. War and disagreement and states and . . . Oh, those are the games we play. Yet we are loving awareness.

We are loving awareness.

REFLECTION ON LOVINGKINDNESS

by Sharon Salzberg

Sharon Salzberg is the master of metta, the practice of love and friendship that is known as "lovingkindness." Sharon is one of the pioneers who brought Buddhist meditation practices to the West from India and Burma. Together with Joseph Goldstein and Jack Kornfield, she cofounded the Insight Meditation Society and later cofounded the Barre Center for Buddhist Studies and the Forest Refuge, a long-term retreat center. She is the author of thirteen books, such as Lovingkindness: The Revolutionary Art of Happiness*;* Real Happiness: The Power of Meditation*; and* Finding Your Way: Meditations, Thoughts, and Wisdom for Living an Authentic Life.

The practice of metta is a way in which we can all be kind to one another, to offer lovingkindness to those we love already and to those we have difficulties with—and to ourselves. Like the Dalai Lama has said, "My religion is kindness." It is a way to break down the boundaries between us *and* them*, to stop seeing the "other" as being so very different from ourselves. After all, what does anyone want but to be safe, to be healthy, to be happy, and to live with ease?*

Lovingkindness. The word in Pali, the language of the original Buddhist texts, is *metta*. There was a time when I really hoped for the word "metta" to enter the culture because I find it so hard to translate. The common translation is "lovingkindness." It is that sense of deeply knowing our lives are connected. We have something to do with one another, and the acknowledgment of that is the sense of metta.

Bob Thurman said to me, "Don't be so timid, just say love, since that's what you actually mean." But that I find very complex, because we can use the word "love" in so many different ways. Why does Ram Dass feel the need to qualify it as unconditional love? It's because sometimes when we talk about love, we frankly mean a medium of exchange. Like, I will love you as long as you love me in return, as long as the following fifteen conditions are met. I will love myself as long as I never make a mistake. We know that state quite well, and we also know its fragility, its vulnerability. So it's not really what we mean by metta, which can sustain us, uphold us, and give us a sense of resiliency, that kind of vast connection, no matter what situation we might be in.

The closest literal translation is "friendship"—a sense of friendship with ourselves and with all beings. We also define friendship in different ways, so I keep coming back to connection. It's this deep knowing that our lives are connected. The corollary to that is that everybody counts. Everybody matters. We're not going to like everybody; we're not going to take everybody home with us; we're not going to give everybody what they want, but everybody matters in some way.

I was teaching a series of daylong workshops in Washington,

DC, and the rental facility was an elementary school, which had the rules of kindness on these big pieces of paper all along the corridors. They included things like "Don't hurt anyone on the inside or on the outside." But my very, very favorite rule of kindness was "Everybody gets to play." Everybody gets to play. Not everybody is your best friend, but everybody gets to play. So that's kind of the sensibility of lovingkindness. Everybody counts. Everybody matters, including oneself.

The companion quality to metta is compassion. Some people define compassion as love which recognizes suffering or adversity. That state of compassion is a kind of tenderness which resonates and responds. It's not just sensing a difficult situation or likely painful situation, but it's an ability to move toward suffering but not being engulfed by it. It's having some sense of perspective or wisdom or equanimity, a balance born of wisdom, which is a perspective that keeps us going in that state of compassion so that we don't get overwhelmed. Ram Dass talked about this when he talked about getting over self-pity in order to have that bigger sense and ability to give.

In a lot of ways, the examples of lovingkindness are metta and compassion. They're often talked about as practices of generosity. Why are we taking time to listen to a stranger rather than thinking about the email we need to send or where we'd rather be? How do we actually arrive at being a real presence and an opening, a sense of open space with a person who's in trouble? We need some kind of resiliency.

Those moments when we really arrive and we are listening and we're open and we care, they're not inconsequential, because they don't last. Sometimes we think, Well, I blew it. But we can come back. That's the essential teaching—we can renew, we can return, we can start over.

The Buddha said, "If you really loved yourself, you'd never harm another." We have such a meager idea of what a human life can be and what we're capable of. But if we really loved ourselves, we would never harm another because it brings us down. We would recognize we've acted out of harmony, feel the pain of that, acknowledge that. In effect, we would forgive ourselves and move on in a really energized way.

It's such a tremendous challenge to us and all the assumptions that we make about happiness, about strength, about love, about ourselves, about others, about "It's a dog-eat-dog world." Why do we make that kind of exploration? Sometimes it is adversity or suffering. Sometimes it's inspiration. And sometimes it's the ability or it's the circumstance. You encounter somebody or something—a place, a work of art, a piece of music, whatever it is—and we see it's a bigger world than we might've imagined. It's like the door blowing open. There is the opportunity to make it real, to embody it, to live it, and as Ram Dass said, to move from *seeing love* to *being love*. That's something we can do. It's not a far-off, nearly impossible goal, although it's likely we can only do it for a few moments and then we forget. But that's okay because we can remember and we can start over.

And that's what practice is—an amazing opportunity to breathe life into something instead of holding it as a kind of abstract value. There are ways we practice sitting or walking meditation. Sometimes we do it through mindfulness. Just pay attention to where you are. Feel your feet against the ground. Look around. And when you see your mind going away, come back to the moment.

In lovingkindness practice, we use phrases as the resting place for one's attention. Bring your energy into your body, eyes open, and silently repeat certain phrases, like "May I be happy; may I be peaceful." I would suggest offering the phrases to yourself as the baseline, then when someone comes strongly into your awareness, include them—"May they be happy"—then go back to resting your attention on the phrases for yourself. You have this touchstone for your awareness that you can lightly be aware of and then play as you expand. When I'm walking down the streets of New York doing metta, every once in a while somebody coming from the other direction gives me a really big smile and I think, Oh, maybe they're doing it too. We've got a little secret love club going on here: metta in action.

Lovingkindness is also born from seeing that all beings want to be happy. Usually we are completely clueless about where happiness is truly to be found. If only you had this or that, then you would be happy. But that urge toward happiness can be aligned with wisdom instead of ignorance, and then it's like a homing instinct for freedom. We can cut through many, many obstacles with that strength. A long time ago, the Dalai Lama said it simply makes sense to develop the happiness of others because then our own chances of happiness "are enhanced six billion to one." Now it's like seven billion to one. He went on to say that those are very good odds.

People often compare lovingkindness meditation to a mantra. Even if you do the recitation in Pali or Sanskrit, it's different from having a seed syllable mantra, such as *om* or *ram*, which is considered to be inherently powerful although we may not know the meaning of it. We do know the meaning of the phrases of lovingkindness, and that's both part of the opportunity and part of the challenge. It isn't an abstract sense of love that we're reflecting on or contemplating. These are beings that we have connection to and fear with and regret about and all kinds of stuff that comes up as we call these beings to mind. It's also used as an opportunity to continually develop more love and compassion for ourselves.

The principle is that the practice is meant to be done in the easiest way possible. It's not the easiest to offer the phrases to yourself, and you may need to start with somebody else, like a benefactor or someone who's helped you. So it's yourself; a benefactor, someone who's helped you or whom you hold in very high regard; a friend; a neutral person like the dry cleaner; a difficult person, somebody you have some conflict with or dis-ease with. Then finally, all beings everywhere.

We also send the phrases out to an "enemy." The enemy doesn't have to be a person. It could be an aspect of oneself, a disease, or even time. It could be suffering itself. Like this shouldn't be here; this is something I want to block or cut off. There are lots of things we can take as an enemy. And in many ways the principles are the same, but it takes a very profound exploration of what it means to have lovingkindness or compassion, say, for a disease. It takes really deep understanding to discern the consequences of enmity, of hatred and fear, which are not very good for us.

Once you have these tools, then there's infinite opportunity to play and adapt and see what works for you and what you might want to do. The most important question is, What are you actually going to put into the practice?

May you be happy.

THE PRACTICE OF METTA (LOVINGKINDNESS)

by Sharon Salzberg

You can sit or lie down comfortably on your back.

Your eyes can be open or closed, however you feel most at ease.

We begin by offering lovingkindness to ourselves by silently repeating phrases:

May I be safe.
May I be happy.
May I be healthy.
May I live with ease.

You can use these phrases or three or four phrases that are meaningful to you. This is like the song of the heart, one phrase at a time with all of your attention gathered behind that one phrase. If you find your attention wandering, don't worry about it or get discouraged. Simply let go of distractions and begin again. Feelings, thoughts, memories may come and go. Allow them to arise and pass away.

Call to mind someone who's helped you, who's been good to you or kind to you. They've inspired you. Say their name to yourself, get a feeling for their presence, and offer the phrases of lovingkindness to them.

Call to mind someone you know who's hurting, who's having a difficult time right now. Say their name to yourself, get a feeling of their presence, and offer the phrases of lovingkindness to them.

Call to mind someone you might encounter now and then—a neighbor, someone you see when you walk your dog. Get a feeling of their presence even though you might not know much or anything about them. We can know that this person wants to be happy just as we do, and we can wish them well.

Call to mind a difficult person, someone whom you have trouble getting along with, or whose words or actions are difficult for you, hard to bear in some way. If it's just too hard to send them lovingkindness, go back to sending lovingkindness to yourself. In that moment, you are the one who's suffering, so you're quite worthy of some compassionate attention.

Then you can offer your well-wishes, the force of lovingkindness, to all beings everywhere. All people, all creatures, all those in existence, known and unknown, near and far. You can direct the force of lovingkindness to all beings in front of you, every form of life, and to either side. All beings behind you, above, and below.

And as you go throughout your day and have various encounters, see if you can actually gather your attention and be there to listen. See if you can pay attention to them quite fully, wishing for their happiness, their well-being, just as you would wish for yourself.

May you be safe.
May you be happy.
May you be healthy.
May you live with ease.

Afterword

AND IN THE END

by Ram Dass

My path is very simple. My path is the path of service and of love—service because there's nothing else I can do, and love because it is such an absolutely royal road through. It's so much easier than the way of *gyan*, the way of knowledge, because all you have to do is love. Maharajji kept saying to me in various ways, "You don't have to change anybody; you just have to love them."

Finally, what you become is an environment, a vibratory rate, which allows others to change. And that's what we do for each other when we're at our clearest. We create an environment where another person can come up for air if they're ready. We never force another person to come up for air because we don't have any moral right to do that. You can't take away another person's suffering. You can create an environment where if they want to let it go, there's nothing in your head that'll keep them stuck in it.

One of Gandhi's strongest lines that guides me all the time

is . . . he's on a train about to leave and a reporter rushes up and says, "Mahatmaji, give me a message to take back to the people in my village." Gandhi just has time to scribble on a piece of paper. It says "My life is my message." Your life is your message. You dwell in love, and everybody who meets you, just by your presence, has an opportunity to come into love. You don't lay a trip, you don't proselytize, you don't prove, and you give people plenty of space. I won't lay a trip on you. I am what I am. A child will hear it. The hardest person will hear it.

Finally, you work on yourself spiritually as an offering to your fellow beings. Because until you have cultivated that quality of peace and equanimity and love and joy and presence and honesty and truth and simplicity, all of your acts are colored by your attachments. You can't wait to be enlightened to act. So you use your acts as ways of working on yourself. *My entire life is my path.*

We are individuals, but there is no *us* or *them*. We are the whole thing. We are those who seek the truth. We are satsang. There is no "other." We are all God. We're all beings together. One consciousness. You are an individual and you are part of the whole. When you finally get to be loving awareness, *be* loving awareness. *Be.*

As Emmanuel, my ghostly friend, said to me, "Ram Dass, why don't you take the curriculum? Try being human." It's an exquisite curriculum. I invite you to join me in matriculating.

Namaste.

Acknowledgments

First and foremost, I am forever indebted to Ram Dass for introducing me to Maharajji and the path of bhakti yoga and for his decades of sharing his love and wisdom and teachings that stem from Maharajji's oft-repeated injunctions to *love everyone*, *serve everyone*, *remember God*, and *tell the truth*.

Many thanks to the Love Serve Remember Foundation for caretaking the Ram Dass archives, and especially to my son Noah Markus, who searched for and provided the relevant talks from the Ram Dass archives for me to do this book, and to Raghu Markus, the director of the LSR Foundation, for shepherding this project along.

Tremendous thanks to Anne Lamott for the foreword, which she originally shared with the Ram Dass Fellowship (https://www.ramdass.org/fellowship), and to Sharon Salzberg, Joseph Goldstein, and Jack Kornfield for their reflections, adapted from podcasts done for the Be Here Now Network (https://beherenownetwork.com).

I was blessed to work with an incredibly insightful editor, Gabriella Page-Fort, the very capable Ryan Amato, and the whole HarperOne team.

Great appreciation to Mirabai Bush, who conceived the idea for this book, and contributed the practice of Just Like Me, to Mirabai Starr for her work on the original outline, and to those who read early drafts and sent valuable feedback: Rameshwar Das, Radha Baum, Nicole Tetreault, and Christina Cagle.

I am grateful to Dylan, Zoey, and Willow—my lovebugs and my hopes for the future.

And as always, eternal thanks to Maharajji, the satguru who allowed me to taste unconditional love.

Source Material from Ram Dass Talks

Sixties

Hollow Bamboo and Purification (Sculpture Studio NYC, NY 3/24/69)

Yale University (New Haven, CT 10/18/69)

Seventies

Growing Out of Dualism (San Francisco, CA, 1970s)

Arlington Street Church (Boston, MA, 3/16/70)

Mackey Auditorium (Boulder, CO, 6/23/74)

Merging with the Divine (Lawrence, KS, 9/26/75)

Shrine Auditorium (Los Angeles, CA, 2/7/76)

Roger Williams Retreat (Roger Williams College, Bristol, CT, 6/14/76)

Relationships and Roles (Caspar, CA, 2/3/78)

Karma Yoga Retreat (Lama Foundation, NM, 1978)

Quiet Mind and Open Heart (Joshua Tree, CA, 1979)

All That Is Not Free (Honolulu, HI, 1/20/79)

Ram Dass Interviewed (8/5/79)

Christian Community of SF (San Francisco, CA, 12/29/79)

From Separation to Source (Myriad Convention Center, Oklahoma City, OK, 1970s)

Eighties

RD - Petaluma (Petaluma, CA, 6/5/81)

Veterans Memorial Auditorium (Santa Rosa, CA, 4/5/82)

Lama Foundation (NM 7/3/82)

Adults and Their Parents (Lama Foundation, NM, 7/13/86)

The Spirit of Service (Lama Foundation, NM, 7/17/86)

Them as Us (11/14/86)

Cultivating the Heart of Compassion (Oklahoma City, OK, 2/25/87)

Cultivating the Heart of Compassion (Los Angeles, CA, 2/1/87)

Where the Path Leads Us (Los Angeles, CA, 2/18/89)

The Listening Heart (9/18/89)

A Day with Ram Dass (Santa Barbara, CA, 4/22/89)

The Practice of Be Here Now (1989)

Ann Arbor (MI, 1980s)

Unlocking the Door (Los Angeles, CA, 1980s)

The Journey to Awakening (New York City, NY, 1980s)

Promises and Pitfalls of the Spiritual Path (Santa Rosa, CA, 1980s)

Social Action/Spiritual Path (Lama Foundation, NM, 1980s)

An Evening with Ram Dass (Santa Barbara, CA, 1980s)

On Relationships (1980s)

On Suffering (1980s)

Nineties

Balance of Heart & Mind (Duke University, NC, 4/13/90)

Life is a Dance (Eugene, OR, 5/23/90)

Findhorn Foundation (1991)

Behind the Changing (Edgartown, MA, 8/9/92)

Working from Within (Syracuse, NY, 3/4/93)

Freedom Through Roles (UC Berkeley, CA, 5/22/93)

Tuning to the Wisdom Heart (Omega Institute, Rhinebeck, NY, 7/22/93)

Escaping the Prison of Separateness (New York City, NY, 5/6/94)

Program 4 (Detroit, OR, 8/23/94)

Behind the Clinging (US Virgin Islands 2/95)

The Presence (1998)

Keeping Relationships Alive (St. Moritz, Switzerland, 1990s)

2000s

Roles and Souls (Maui, HI, 2010)

Fear of Judgment (Maui, HI, 2010)

OYHIP Retreat 2011 (Maui, HI, 12/7/11)

Notes

Introduction by Parvati Markus

3 *Hippies create police; police create hippies:* Ram Dass, *Be Here Now* (Hanuman Foundation, 1978), 27–28.

Chapter 1: "Us" Versus "Them"

24 *Our normal waking consciousness:* William James, *The Varieties of Religious Experience: A Study in Human Nature* (Longmans, Green & Co., 1902).

25 *Father, there is little to tell:* "Anandamayi Ma—The 'Blissful Mother,'" 360° Hinduism, https://360hinduism.com/cover-story-anandamayi-ma-the-blissful-mother.

Chapter 2: From Judgment to Appreciation

36 *Timothy Leary said, "I'm tired of being should upon":* Ram Dass and Rameshwar Das, *Polishing the Mirror: How to Live from Your Spiritual Heart* (Sounds True, 2013), 221.

Chapter 5: Time to Go Home

107 *If I am not at home anywhere in the universe:* Ram Dass and Rameshwar Das, *Polishing the Mirror: How to Live from Your Spiritual Heart* (Sounds True, 2013), 122.

Chapter 7: From Role to Soul

141 *This body has lived with father, mother, husband, and all*: "Anandamayi Ma—The 'Blissful Mother,'" 360° Hinduism, https://360hinduism.com/cover-story-anandamayi-ma-the-blissful-mother.

Chapter 8: Be Here Now

153 *At first it was an adventure:* Ram Dass and Rameshwar Das, *Being Ram Dass* (Sounds True, 2021), 165.

164 *Birth is thus, death is thus, verse or no verse, what's the fuss?:* A haiku by Dahui Zonggao found in Ta Hui, *Swampland Flowers: The Letters and Lectures of Zen Master Ta Hui*, trans. J. C. Cleary (Grove Press, 1977), xvii.

Reflection on Compassion and Equanimity by Joseph Goldstein

172 *Once the realization is accepted:* Rainer Maria Rilke, *Rilke on Love and Other Difficulties*, trans. John J. L. Mood (W. W. Norton & Company, 1994).

The Practice of Meditation by Ram Dass

180 *"There seems no centre because it is all centre":* C. S. Lewis, *Perelandra* (Collier Books, 1962).

Chapter 9: The Teachers—Everyone and Everything

186 *If you see everything in the universe:* Ram Dass and Rameshwar Das, *Polishing the Mirror: How to Live from your Spiritual Heart* (Sounds True, 2013), 19.

Chapter 10: The Community of Spiritual Seekers

204 *We have to take refuge in our sangha:* Remarks from Thich Nhat Hanh to over two thousand people attending his Day of Mindfulness at Spirit Rock Center in Woodacre, California, in October 1993. Thich Nhat Hanh, "The Next Buddha May Be a Sangha," *Inquiring Mind* 10, no. 2 (Spring 1994), https://inquiringmind.com/article/1002_41_thich-nhat_hanh.

Chapter 11: God, Guru, Self

217 *There is no difference between God, Guru, and Self:* Ramana Maharshi, *The Teachings of Bhagavan Sri Ramana Maharshi in His Own Words*, ed. Arthur Osborne (Sri Ramanasramam Tiruvannamalai, 2002), 86.

Chapter 12: Wholeness and Loving Awareness

237 *Since the day when I met with my Lord:* Kabir, Poem 41, *Songs of Kabir*, trans. Rabindranath Tagore (MacMillan Co., 1915).

About the Author

Ram Dass, one of America's most beloved spiritual figures, made his mark on the world by teaching the path of the heart (bhakti yoga), and promoting service (seva) and care for the dying. Ram Dass first went to India in 1967, when he was still Dr. Richard Alpert, a former psychology professor at Harvard and a psychedelic pioneer with Dr. Timothy Leary. In India, he met his guru, Neem Karoli Baba, affectionately known as Maharajji, who gave Ram Dass his name, which means "servant of God."

On his return from India, Ram Dass became a pivotal influence on a culture that has reverberated ever since with the words "be here now," also the title of his iconic 1971 publication. Even after a devastating stroke, he carried on, writing books and sharing loving awareness with both individuals and groups who met with him either in person or online in heart-to-heart talks.

Ram Dass's spirit has been a guiding light for four generations, carrying millions along on the journey and helping to free them from their bonds. With *There Is No Other*, Ram Dass's essential guidance is gathered together to help us heal our divisions and create wholeness in our lives.

He left his body in 2019 at his home in Maui.

About the Editor

Parvati Markus is the editor of *Dying to Know: Ram Dass & Timothy Leary*; and the author of *Whisper in the Heart: The Ongoing Presence of Neem Karoli Baba*; *Love Everyone: The Transcendent Wisdom of Neem Karoli Baba Told Through the Stories of the Westerners Whose Lives He Transformed*; and coauthor of a children's book, *Isabella Castaspella*, which is in development as an animated series called *Izzy Casts a Spell*.

Parvati is a developmental editor who has been midwifing spiritually oriented nonfiction books and memoirs since she first met Ram Dass in 1969 and helped with Ram Dass's classic *Be Here Now*. She has served with spiritual organizations (as past president of the board of the Neem Karoli Baba Ashram and Temple in Taos, New Mexico) and events (as a development consultant for the Global Peace Initiative of Women), and is on the Advisor Circle for the Love Serve Remember Foundation.

Parvati lives in Los Angeles, enjoying the nearby presence of her sons and granddaughters.